Imperial Citizen

Gender and Globalization
Susan S. Wadley, *Series Editor*

Other titles from Gender and Globalization

Family, Gender, and Law in a Globalizing Middle East and South Asia
Kenneth M. Cuno and Manisha Desai, eds.

From Patriarchy to Empowerment: Women's Participation, Movements, and Rights in the Middle East, North Africa, and South Asia
Valentine M. Moghadam, ed.

Hijab and the Republic: Uncovering the French Headscarf Debate
Bronwyn Winter

La Chulla Vida: Gender, Migration, and the Family in Andean Ecuador and New York City
Jason Pribilsky

Making Miss India Miss World: Constructing Gender, Power, and the Nation in Postliberalization India
Susan Dewey

Policing Egyptian Women: Sex, Law, and Medicine in Khedival Egypt
Liat Kozma

Transforming Faith: The Story of Al-Huda and Islamic Revivalism among Urban Pakistani Women
Sadaf Ahmad

Imperial Citizen

Marriage and Citizenship in the Ottoman Frontier Provinces of Iraq

Karen M. Kern

SYRACUSE UNIVERSITY PRESS

Syracuse, New York 13244-5290

First Edition 2011
11 12 13 14 15 16 6 5 4 3 2 1

Portions of Selim's letter to Isma'il appeared in *The Islamic World.* William H. McNeill and Marilyn Robinson Waldman, eds.; John E. Woods, trans. Chicago: Univ. of Chicago Press, 1973, pp. 338–42. Reprinted here with permission.

∞ The paper used in this publication meets the minimum requirements of the American National Standard for Information Sciences—Permanence of Paper for Printed Library Materials, ANSI Z39.48-1992.

For a listing of books published and distributed by Syracuse University Press, visit our Web site at SyracuseUniversityPress.syr.edu.

ISBN: 978-0-8156-3285-6

Library of Congress Cataloging-in-Publication Data
Kern, Karen M.
Imperial citizen : marriage and citizenship in the Ottoman frontier provinces of Iraq / Karen M. Kern. — 1st ed.
p. cm. — (Gender and globalization)
Includes bibliographical references and index.
ISBN 978-0-8156-3285-6 (cloth : alk. paper)
1. Marriage law—Turkey—History. 2. Marriage law—Iraq—History. 3. Citizenship—Turkey. 4. Impediments to marriage—Turkey. 5. Impediments to marriage—Iraq. 6. Sunnites—Relations—Shi'ah. 7. Shi'ah—Relations—Sunnites. I. Title.
KKX544.K47 2011
346.56101'6—dc23 2011034039

Manufactured in the United States of America

Karen M. Kern is an associate professor in the Department of History at Hunter College, The City University of New York. She is the author of a number of articles on citizenship, Ottoman law, and women and family history. She is also the recipient of a number of awards and fellowships, including the J. William Fulbright Foreign Scholarship Board and the U.S. Department of State Certificate of Recognition in 2002; The City of New York "Salute to Scholars" Certificate of Recognition in 2001; and the Fulbright Senior Researcher Fellowship in 2000.

Contents

Acknowledgments

Imperial Citizen is the result of many years of research and writing that were made enjoyable by the encouragement of my family and many friends and colleagues. I owe a debt of gratitude to all of them for their personal and professional support.

This book came to fruition under the guidance and encouragement of my advisors Jeanette Wakin and Kathleen Burrill in the Department of Middle East, South Asian, and African Studies at Columbia University. Their collaboration and guidance throughout my studies was unwavering and truly appreciated. My deep appreciation, similarly, goes to George Saliba and Richard Bulliet for their enthusiasm throughout the process of researching and writing this book. I also wish to thank Nader Sohrabi, the organizer of the Turkish Studies Seminar at Columbia University, for giving me the opportunity to present this work and benefit from the thoughtful comments of the seminar members. I am particularly grateful to the anonymous readers of this manuscript for their insightful comments and criticisms, which allowed me to think more clearly about the broader issues raised in this book.

I am grateful to the staff of the Başbakanlık Osmanlı Arşivi for their excellent service and assistance in tracking down documents. I also wish to thank all of my colleagues from the archives whose advice and friendship contributed to the enjoyable and exciting experience of working on Ottoman history at the center of this world in Istanbul. I send my appreciation to Snjezana Buzov, Radha Dalal, Yücel Demirel, Selim Deringil, Caroline Finkel, Benjamin Fortna, Shirine Hamadeh, Charles Haley, Yavuz Karakışla, Nicole Van Os, Fariba Zarinebaf, Selma Zecevic, and Cangüzel Zülfikar.

For the friends I met along the way—Iris Agmon, Meltem Ahıska, Nejat Çınar, David Cuthell, Ali Erdemci, Neşe Ersoz, Timuçin Gürer, Charlotte Jirousek, Rama Keilani, Sheila Matthews, Janet Molzan Turan, Lucienne Şenocak, Mehmet Taygun, and Hale Tenger—thank you for your companionship, which allowed me to experience Turkey in ways that would have been impossible without you.

This research was supported by grants from the Fulbright Commission. I am grateful for the opportunity they provided to spend extended periods of time on my research. My deep appreciation is extended to Fulbright's executive director, Professor Ersin Onulduran, and the staff in Istanbul and Ankara. The Istanbul branch of the American Research Institute in Turkey has been my home away from home for many years. I thank Tony Greenwood, Gülden Guneri, and Semrin Korkmaz for their hospitality and generous assistance in providing the atmosphere that allows scholars to flourish.

Finally, I am most indebted to my brother, John Kern, who encouraged me from the inception of this project, and to my father and mother, Louis J. Kern and Edith C. Kern, who never doubted, and always supported, my choices in life. This book is dedicated to them.

A Note on Transliteration

This study of Ottoman centralization and frontier policies as applied in the three eastern provinces that compose modern day Iraq required utilization of both the Arabic and Turkish languages. Wherever terms refer to the Ottoman administration or to titles and proper names of persons of Turkish origins, these words have been transliterated using modern Turkish. Terms that refer to local Arabic administration and titles are rendered in Arabic transliteration.

Arabic: All diacritical marks are omitted, except

ʿ	ayn
ʾ	hamza

Turkish pronunciation:

C, c	"j" as in "jury"
Ç, ç	"ch" as in "chief"
Ğ, ğ	soft "g" usually not pronounced, but lengthens the preceding vowel
I, ı	undotted I, pronounced like "ea" as in "early"
İ, i	dotted "i" as in "in"
Ö, ö	as the umlaut "ö" in German
Ş, ş	"sh" as in "shift"
Ü, ü	as the umlaut "ü" in German

Abbreviations

AHR	*The American Historical Review*
A.MKT.MHM	Sadaret Mektubi Kalemi Mühimme Kalemi Odası Belgeleri, BOA
ASR	*American Sociological Review*
BOA	Başbakanlık Osmanlı Arşivi
CS	*Citizenship Studies*
CSSH	*Comparative Studies in Society and History*
DH.H	Dahiliye Nezareti Hukuk Kısım Belgeleri, BOA
DH.HMŞ	Dahiliye Nezareti Hukuk Müşavirliği Belgeleri, BOA
DH.İD	Dahiliye Nezareti İdari Kısım Belgeleri, BOA
DH.İUM	Dahiliye Nezareti İdare-i Umumiye Belgeleri, BOA
DH.MB.HPS.M	Dahiliye Nezareti Mebani-i Emiriye ve Hapishaneler Müdüriyeti Belgeleri (İdare Kalemi), BOA
DH.MUİ	Dahiliye Nezareti Muhaberat-ı Umumiye İdaresi Belgeleri, BOA
DH.SN.THR	Dahiliye Nezareti Sicill-i Nüfus İdare-i Umumiyesi Belgeleri (Tahrirat Kalemi), BOA
DH.SYS	Dahiliye Nezareti Siyasi Kısım Belgeleri, BOA
EI	*Encyclopedia Iranica*
HIA-HDC	Hoover Institution Archives, Hidayet Dağdeviren Collection

HR.HMŞ.İŞO	Hukuk Müşavirliği İştişare Odası Belgeleri, BOA
IJMES	*International Journal of Middle East Studies*
IS	*Iranian Studies*
JAOS	*Journal of the American Oriental Society*
MES	*Middle Eastern Studies*
M.V.	Meclis-i Vükela Mazbataları, BOA
Y.A.HUS	Yıldız Sadaret Hususı Maruzat Evrakı, BOA
Y.A.RES	Yıldız Sadaret Resmi Maruzat Evrakı, BOA
Y.MTV	Yıldız Mütenevvi Maruzat Evrakı, BOA

Imperial Citizen

Introduction

THIS BOOK is an examination of how the Ottoman Empire adopted and adapted the concepts of nationality and citizenship to the geopolitical exigencies of controlling its easternmost frontier provinces in Iraq during the final fifty years of its existence. The constraint that defined these concepts, rhetorically, was the centuries-old rivalry between the Ottoman and Iranian states, which was based on the historic Sunni-Shiʿi schism. Although couched in religious rhetoric, this division had tangible religious, political, legal, and economic implications for Ottoman policies in the Iraqi provinces, and for Ottoman and Iranian relations.

Ottoman constructions of nationality and citizenship were part of the centralizing policies of the Tanzimat Reforms. These concepts became important components in the definition of Ottoman-Iranian relations in the latter decades of the empire, particularly where they concerned control of the eastern frontier provinces of Mosul, Baghdad, and Basra—three provinces that would come to make up modern Iraq. The main framework for this book is a specific aspect of Ottoman citizenship law, which prohibited marriages between Ottoman women and Iranian men—a prohibition that Ottoman officials perceived as an integral part of their effort to maintain and control the three eastern provinces. A marriage prohibition between Sunnis and Shiʿites had a long history in the Ottoman Empire, going back to the sixteenth century when the Safavids established control over Iran. The Safavid and later Qajar-Shiʿite states, and their influence in Ottoman territory, were considered a threat to Ottoman control over the Iraqi provinces. The prohibition of marriages between Sunnis and Shiʿites was the space in which the Ottomans fought an ideological and rhetorical battle over political and territorial spheres of influence.

The rhetorical language of religious division, the Sunni-Shiʿi schism, was the foundation for the marriage prohibition in the sixteenth century. This schism continued to be utilized through the centuries and well into the final decades of the Ottoman Empire. The intention of the prohibition was to suppress an increase of the Shiʿite population in the frontier regions. By the final decades of the nineteenth century, Ottoman officials also preserved the prohibition on the basis of national difference, but it is clear from the discussions in the Cabinet and in the various ministries that the quarrel between these two states was still one over differences in religious dogma, which was used to support polices in contested spheres of political and territorial influence.

In recent years, historians of political, diplomatic, and economic history have produced a vast number of seminal studies on the history of the Ottoman Empire from the Tanzimat Reforms until the empire's collapse, from the perspective of both the central administration and the Arab provinces.[1] Historians today also have at their disposal a number of important comprehensive histories of Iraq utilizing British and Arab sources, which complement studies on the history of Iraqi politics and economy that use both Arab and Ottoman archival sources.[2]

This book does not attempt a comprehensive examination of late nineteenth- or early twentieth-century Iraqi history. While this study is firmly planted within the growing body of literature on the Ottoman eastern provinces of Iraq, it focuses particularly on Ottoman centralization policies as officials attempted to extend their authority in this border region at a time when it was threatened by both European expansion and unstable relations with its near neighbor, Iran. This study pushes the field forward by exploring the connection between Ottoman centralizing policies and the

1. To mention just a few works, see Findley 1980; Cleveland 1985; Hanioğlu 1995 and 2001; Deringil 1998; Quataert 2000; Karpat 2001; Somel 2001; Fortna 2002; and Finkel 2005. For history of the Arab provinces, see Ochsenwald 1984; Akarlı 1993; Messick 1993; Rogan 1999; Makdisi 2000; Thompson 2000; Massad 2001; and Mundy and Smith 2007.

2. For comprehensive histories, see Marr 1985; Nakash 1994; Anscombe 1997; Litvak 1998; and Tripp 2000. On Iraqi politics and economy under the Ottoman Empire, see Fattah 1997; Khoury 1997; Shields 2000; and Çetinsaya 2006.

role of nationality and gender in the construction of the new concept of citizenship. Recent examinations of the frontier provinces of the Ottoman Empire have had little to say about the relationship between centralizing policies and the institution of marriage (Messick 1993; Deringil 1998; Najmabadi 1998; Rogan 1999; Akiba 2000; Hanssen, Philipp, and Weber 2002).[3] Marriage had an important demographic component because it had a variety of social and economic effects on the fabric of society. The institution reached into the very heart of public order and moral behavior, and, as a result, central management of marriage became an important element in the control of the population on the peripheries in the Iraqi provinces. This book, therefore, is the first in-depth examination of the intersection of Ottoman centralizing policies and nationality and citizenship law, and their effects on the demographic component of marriage in the frontier provinces of Iraq.

The research for this study is based on documents in the Ottoman state archives as well as published and unpublished materials. It is important to mention that classification and release of archival materials is an ongoing process, and, therefore, it is always possible to return to the archives and discover additional documents on this topic. Repeated trips to the archives over the past few years have yielded many more documents on the topic of the prohibition of marriages between Ottoman women and Iranian men, and related materials associated with this subject, which are discussed in this book. These documents have occasionally clarified questions that have arisen during research but, to date, have not substantially altered the analysis and findings in this book.

Before discussing the division of chapters, it is necessary to examine a number of key concepts that are essential to analyzing the demographic importance of marriage for Ottoman centralization policies in the provinces of Iraq. We will consider the two theories of nationalism and of citizenship, which have been treated for many decades in numerous studies

3. Other important recent articles concerning Ottoman frontier policies include Rogan 1996; Kühn 2002 and 2003; Makdisi 2002b; Blumi 2003a and 2003b; and Deringil 2003.

across cultures but have not been well analyzed in the Ottoman imperial context. The third concept is the notion of the frontier, which is a growing area of research for scholars of Ottoman history, but little studied for the Ottoman Iraqi provinces. We will, finally, discuss a theoretical framework for the demographic component of marriage, to highlight its importance to Ottoman control over its eastern frontier provinces.

It is necessary to make some remarks on the usage of term "Iraq" in this book. In the last decades of the nineteenth century, we find references in Ottoman archival documents to "Iraq," but more generally the Ottomans referred to their eastern frontier provinces as "Baghdad," "Basra," and "Mosul."[4] The name Iraq was not utilized to refer to a territory until after World War I, when the three Ottoman provinces fell under the British Mandate. In recent years, it has become a convention among scholars of Ottoman history to use the term "Ottoman Iraq" for the three provinces (Nieuwenhuis 1982; Fattah 1997; Çetinsaya 2006). For the purposes of simplicity, the terms "Ottoman Iraq" or "Iraq" are used throughout this book for the geographical area that made up the three Ottoman provinces of Baghdad, Basra, and Mosul. It is also important to note that most of the discussion in the book concerns two of the Ottoman provinces, Baghdad and Basra. Because Mosul was largely a Kurdish area with different sociopolitical structures, it was the subject of different Ottoman concerns than those specific to the two provinces to its south. Where there are interconnections, Mosul will also be mentioned. But for the issues concerned in this book, Mosul demands a separate study.

Nationalism and Citizenship from the Tanzimat Reforms to the End of Empire

The body of literature on nationalism is vast and spans the academic disciplines. Scholars have developed many general theories on the meaning

4. See Çetinsaya 2006, 1, for example, who quotes a memorandum from Abdüllatif Suphi Paşa to Sultan Abdülaziz in 1864 where he discusses "the productive capacity of the land in the provinces of Syria and Iraq," among other matters concerning the Arab provinces.

of nationalism as a part of modern history, but there is no consensus. Current scholarship is still concerned with the broadest questions, such as the definition of *the nation* and *nationalism,* and the mechanisms for nation-formation.[5] Broad questions—such as how nationalism produces the modern nation state—do not fundamentally address how nationalism is presented and utilized in a nineteenth-century imperial context.

The few studies that have examined the rise of nationalism in the Ottoman Empire have left us with more questions than answers. The issue is certainly very complex.[6] Some scholars have focused on an abstract ideology known as *Ottomanism (Osmanlılık)* as evidence of the spread of nationalism (White 1999, 79). Ottomanism was, in fact, a formulation of imperial identity that appeared partially in response to growing nationalist sentiments in the Balkan territories. It was a strategy developed by intellectuals such as Namık Kemal, whose goal was to create a type of national unity among a population of many ethnicities and religions. The concept was firmly rooted in the person of the sultan, and therefore lacked the kind of emotional and cultural attachments common in European concepts of nationhood.

Scholars have examined the impact of this ideology on the Ottoman elite, and have maintained that Ottomanism was evidence of national-identity formation (Kuran 1968; Lewis 1964 and 1968). A number of difficulties exist in studying nationalism as an ideology. It is not easy, for example, to discover the conditions through which these ideas were transferred outside of elite society and entered the consciousness of the

5. See Dahbour and Ishay 1995 and Suny and Eley 1996 for a compilation of authors and their writings on nationalism. See Thompson and Fevre 2001 for a comprehensive discussion of the main developments in sociology on the nation and nationalism.

6. See 2002 "Special Issue: Nationalism and the Colonial Legacy in the Middle East and Central Asia," *IJMES* 34, no. 2 for numerous articles about the formation of post-imperial nationalism and nation state formation. For an important study of the state of scholarship on nationalism in the Middle East and the need for comparative analysis see Behar 2005. For the Ottoman Empire, see Anderson 1994; Quataert 2000, particularly pp. 68–71; and Salzmann 1999.

nonelite social classes and diverse ethnic and religious communities in both the central and peripheral regions. If one can establish a mechanism to analyze this transfer, can one find where a shift occurred from religious and ethnic allegiances to an abstract ideology that called for primary loyalty to the imperial dynasty? In the past, this approach has ignored the role of local factors in reinforcing, or subverting, national-identity formation. To make the matter of defining nationalism in the Ottoman context even more difficult, many recent studies share the argument that nationalism did not truly gain momentum as a social phenomenon before the collapse of the Ottoman Empire (Cleveland 1985, 24; Dawn 1991, 3–31; Quataert 2000, 68–71; Özoğlu 2001, 383–86). These studies argue that the emergence of nationalism was the result of Ottoman collapse, and not a cause for the end of the empire.

In examining nationalism in the Ottoman context, it is useful to consider John Breuilly's argument that

> to focus upon culture, ideology, identity, class or modernization is to neglect the fundamental point that nationalism is, above and beyond all else, about politics and politics is about power. Power, in the modern world, is primarily about control of the state. The central question, therefore, should be to relate nationalism to the objective of obtaining and using state power. (1982, 1–2)

Although Breuilly's quote reflects his thinking about the modern nation state, his emphasis on nationalism as a mechanism of power politics is relevant to this examination of Ottoman imperial nationalism. He defines *nationalism* as a "political movement seeking or exercising state power and justifying such actions with nationalist arguments" (1982, 3). As will be shown throughout this study, one of the main goals of intellectuals in constructing the ideology of Ottomanism was to create loyal subjects who would accept the state's extensive centralization policies.[7] The interests

7. A few recent examples of scholarship that shows the complexity of local nationalisms in the Ottoman Empire include Christophoros 2006 on divisions within Albanian

and values of the centralizing state took priority over local concerns in the peripheral borderlands of the empire, such as the three eastern provinces that made up Ottoman Iraq. The Ottoman government was not always successful in implementing its policies. Recent studies have shown that even though the central government enacted an extensive program of centralization throughout the empire, minority power bases still remained, with their own definition of ethnic nationalism that conflicted with the broad-based imperial nature of Ottomanism.

To further understand the complexity inherent in Ottoman plans to create an imperial nationalism, it is useful to consider Hugh Seton-Watson's concept of "official nationalism." Official nationalism was common among nineteenth-century dynastic powers such as the Habsburgs, Romanovs, and Ottomans, who attempted to create a "willed merger of nation and dynastic empire."[8] Fuad Paşa, the Ottoman foreign minister, clearly defined a version of Ottoman official nationalism in the 1860s when he was sent to Syria to investigate and punish those responsible for massacres among the Maronites and Druze in Mount Lebanon, and the Christians in Damascus. He described the imperial basis of Ottoman nationalism and reaffirmed the hierarchy of relationships between the dynasty and its subjects. All Ottoman subjects were united by loyalty to the sultan, who upheld the hierarchical social order by treating all with equality and equanimity. For Ottoman officials, Tanzimat-era Ottomanism was defined by loyalty and obedience to the dynasty, which was a

---

nationalist movements at the time of the 1908 revolution; Özoğlu 2001 and Klein 2007 on the lack of unity in the Kurdish national movement; Köksal 2008 on identity formation among local communities in Ankara and Edirne; Makdisi 2002a on official and local views of nationalism in Mount Lebanon after the 1860 disturbances; and Sencer 2004 on the struggles of Macedonian nationalists in the Ottoman Parliament in 1909 to articulate a Balkan nationalism against pressure to maintain at least a rhetorical loyalty to Ottoman official nationalism.

8. See Seton-Watson 1977, chapters 4 and 6; and Anderson 1994, chapter 6, particularly p. 86.

"metaphor of the nation" (Makdisi 2002a, 606).[9] Post-1860 Tanzimat-era Ottomanism was as much about power and politics as about ideology: in this case both the restatement of the sultan's demand for loyalty from his subjects and the power of the Ottoman state to control rebellious regions in the Arab provinces (Berkes 1964).

The long reign of Sultan Abdülhamid II (1876–1909) ushered in an emphasis on pan-Islamism, which was aimed at creating a unity among the Muslim population and preserving the empire despite tremendous territorial losses.[10] This was not an abandonment of official imperial nationalism. At the end of the nineteenth century, Sultan Abdülhamid II sought to reaffirm the legitimacy of the dynasty by reinforcing Islamic legitimacy

9. Scholars who have studied the influence of the ideas of the French Revolution on the Ottoman Empire have disagreed about exactly when the idea of "nation" gained acceptance among the elite. Bernard Lewis and Ercümend Kuran have both noted that, as early as the 1790s, Ottoman ambassadors to the French Directoire and to London were using the word *vatan* in the sense of *patrie* (see Kuran 1968, 109, note 3; also Lewis 1968, 334–35). Fatih Yeşil's research on the writings of Ebubekir Ratib Efendi, the Ottoman ambassador to Vienna from February to July 1792, notes that he was the first Ottoman official to use the terms *millet* and *vatan* with reference to France. *Millet* and *vatan* did not mean a modern nation but a community based on a common religion. For empires with mixed populations, the ambassador used the terms *kavim* or *akvam,* for different ethnic groups (see Yeşil 2007, 301–2). Niyazi Berkes has suggested that it was not until the 1830s and 1840s that even a suggestion can be made that the nationalist ideologies that came out of the French Revolution had an influence on Ottoman or Muslim writers. Even then, he maintains, a direct connection cannot be established. By the middle of the nineteenth century, however, notions of *vatan* were commonplace in government rhetoric and in the society at large. For example, the Gülhane Rescript of 1839 (*Hatt-ı Şerif-i Gülhane)* speaks of love of country (*vatan),* referring to all Ottoman subjects regardless of religion. *Vatan* was being widely used in the Turkish press. In 1866 there was also a newspaper called *The Mirror of the Fatherland* (*Ayine-i Vatan)* (see Lewis 1968, 334–35).

10. By 1830, Greece had become independent from the Ottoman Empire and the French had occupied Algeria. Russia defeated the Ottoman Empire in 1878, which resulted in the loss of Serbia, Rumania, Montenegro, Bosnia, Herzegovina, and Cyprus. The British occupied Egypt in 1882, and there were further losses of Ottoman territory to Greece in 1881 (see Duguid 1973, 139; Deringil 1998, 47).

in the person of the sultan, with the emphasis on his role as caliph. He did this by emphasizing the fundamental dogma of the Hanafi School of Islamic jurisprudence—the official school of the Ottoman Empire—as a means to bring unorthodox and non-Sunni branches of Islam into the mainstream. Abdülhamid, and many of the conservative elites who surrounded him, were concerned with the secularizing tendencies represented by the French positivists, who held sway over leading intellectuals such as Namık Kemal—one of the founders of Ottomanism. Süleyman Hüsnü Paşa, a military officer exiled to Baghdad in 1878, was a part of the conservative Ottoman elite. He wrote a report suggesting ways to bring unorthodox sects into Sunni Islam. He noted the multireligious and multiethnic quality of the Baghdad province, which was composed of Turks, Kurds, Arabs, Chaldeans, Nestorians, Armenians, and Jews, and remarked that Sunni Islam was in the minority. This situation could be redeemable, Süleyman Hüsnü Paşa averred, if the Hamidian regime would create schools to educate non-Sunni subjects in the fundamentals of the religion, and send out Ottoman missionaries to preach to the tribes. The official imperial nationalism of the Hamidian regime required creating a loyal population out of disparate ethnicities, a population also steeped in the correct fundamentals of Sunni Islam (Deringil 1998, 217–21; Fortna 2002, 63–67).

The meaning of official imperial nationalism became more fluid in the post-Hamidian period. During the rule of the Committee of Union and Progress (CUP), opportunities opened for more diverse definitions of imperial nationalism. Conflicting definitions appeared in debates in the Parliament over the lack of law and order in the Macedonian provinces. Muslim deputies from the Balkans insisted on reestablishing law and order for the protection of the unity of the empire, while non-Muslims preferred reform and reorganization of the laws. Early in CUP rule, in January of 1909, Muslim deputies continued to express loyalty to the "official imperial nationalism" of the empire, while the rhetoric of non-Muslim deputies suggested a more nationalist tendency based on their ethnicity, religion, and language. When pressured by challenges from Muslim deputies, however, non-Muslims reaffirmed their loyalty to the notion of Ottoman unity. After the Hamidian period, the space opened for more varying loyalties, particularly in those provinces of the Balkans that remained within the empire. The shift from Ottomanism to Turkism remains one of the most challenging subjects for scholars of this period. In the parliamentary debates of January, 1909, Muslim deputies used the word "Turk," which showed a national consciousness not exhibited by non-Muslims, who continued to use the word "Ottoman." It is difficult to know the degree to which Muslim deputies' affirmation of their allegiance to Ottoman unity was based on continued loyalty to the idea of Ottomanism and to the dynasty, or whether it had been transformed into a more ethnic, Turkish loyalty. Non-Muslim deputies' profession of loyalty to the Ottoman state must also be questioned, because they were clearly under pressure from Muslims deputies to show their allegiance to the state. To date, scholars working in the field concur that the Turkification policy of the CUP was not implemented at this early stage and did not become operational until after 1913 (Sencer 2004; Ülker 2005).

Just as no conclusive definition of "the nation" exists, scholars across disciplines have not developed a coherent theory that encapsulates the definition of "citizenship." Discussions among scholars of the meaning of citizenship began in the middle decades of the twentieth century as a result of the appearance of one of the classic texts on the historical sociology of citizenship: T. H. Marshall's 1949 essay, "Citizenship and Social Class."[11] Marshall established a framework for defining citizenship in Western democratic nations when he posited three stages in the development of citizenship. *Civil citizenship* appeared in the eighteenth century and established the rights of individuals to liberty and justice; to freedom of speech, thought, and religion; and to the right to own property. *Political citizenship,* emerged in the nineteenth century and extended individual rights to participate in political decision-making through appointment

11. The standard theorists of citizenship in the twentieth century include Marshall 1950 and 1965, chapter 4, 71–134; Mann 1987, 339–54; and Turner 1990, 189–217, and 2000, 28–48; Tilly 1995a, 1–17, and 1995b, 223–36. See also Janowitz 1980, 1–24; and van Gunsteren 1994, 47.

or election to institutions with political authority. *Social citizenship* was achieved in the twentieth century and extended to citizens the benefits of social and economic welfare. According to Marshall, an individual's full participation as a citizen would be realized with the establishment of social citizenship. Social citizenship was, therefore, the end of the "history of citizenship." Marshall's examination was firmly directed toward the capitalist societies that developed out of struggles with the *ancien régime.* These struggles were eventually to create political equalities in societies that were separated into economic classes (1950, 1965, 71–134).[12]

Marshall's theory was important for its time and influenced the work of scholars in the United States who were developing analytical models for ethnic and race relations, and for scholars in Britain who were concerned with postwar national welfare (Turner 1990, 190–95). His theory was not, however, the end of the history of citizenship. Critiques of his work, and new theories, continued to unfold during the last half of the twentieth century and into the twenty-first. Michael Mann criticized Marshall's ethnocentricity and illustrated how Marshall's theory was limited to England and was not an appropriate analytical tool for other nations. Mann attempted to develop a more comparative framework that would include monarchies and constitutional regimes. He designated five types of historical citizenship—liberal, reformist, authoritarian monarchist, fascist, and authoritarian socialist. Each of these regime types was confronted with the increasing political power of the bourgeoisie and urban working classes during the rise of industrial capitalism. Mann's discussion of the authoritarian monarchist category was confined to Germany, Austria, Russia, and Japan, but it would also be the closest fit for the Ottoman Empire. These powers, while absolutist, nevertheless had to deal with regional and local power bases held by corporate groups, merchants, and guild associations. In the nineteenth century, they used policies of divide and rule, as well as selective repression and corporate negotiation (Mann 1987, 342; Turner 1990, 195–97). Eventually these monarchies understood that selective reforms were necessary in order to

12. See also Janowitz 1980, 3–4; Mann 1987, 339–40; and van Steenbergen 1994, 3.

modernize their empires. Mann focused on Wilhelmine Germany as a model of an absolutist monarchy that realized the necessity for incorporating regional and local vested interests into the political structure in order to become a "modern" regime and attain Great Power status. In order to achieve this status, the Prussians were willing to grant civil citizenship, including property and labor rights, to the bourgeoisie, but only minimal political and social citizenship. Elected representatives only had limited legislative power, and there was little absolute freedom of the press, speech, or assembly (Mann 1987, 344–49).

Bryan S. Turner agreed with Mann's criticism of Marshall's ethnocentricity, but also critiqued Mann, contending that he was analytically vague. He noted Mann's contribution to the discussion of citizenship, and acknowledged it as an important advancement over Marshall's model, but he criticized Mann on three points. Turner first noted that Mann's analysis was based on class relations and ignored other forms of racial and ethnic social stratification. Mann's work, for example, excluded meaningful discussion of citizenship in countries like Canada, New Zealand, Australia, and the United States, which were composed of mixed racial and ethnic populations. Turner, secondly, observed that Mann ignored the importance of religion and politics during state formation. Turner particularly highlighted the impact of Christianity and Islam in "providing universalist discourse of political space (the City of god and the Household of Islam) that challenged ethnicity and kinship as the primordial ties of the societal community" (1990, 197–99, 212). Turner finally criticized Mann's conception of citizenship as a ruling-class strategy in which citizenship was given by the state and created social integration. Turner noted that Mann did not consider citizenship as a consequence of social struggle over resources. Turner's conception of citizenship was based on the "revolutionary implications of the oppositional character of rights" (1990, 199–212). He attempted to take the discussion away from Marshall's Anglophile focus and continue Mann's discussion of the historical sociology of citizenship. By doing so, Turner proposed that different types of citizenship status which related to gender, age, and race were historically relevant to a discussion of the emergence of citizenship. He highlighted two other arenas that were absent from Mann's discussion—the public and private division in Western cultures, and the distinction between passive and active versions of citizenship. Turner's contribution further developed a theory of citizenship in service of scholars who wished to analyze the problems of modern citizenship.[13]

The Ottomans' notion of citizenship, created within the framework of the official nationalism of Ottomanism, does not fit neatly into Marshall's Western-based categories. Michael Mann's discussion of citizenship under absolutist monarchies has more in common with the Ottoman experience in establishing its version of citizenship. Although Mann's analysis was class-based and did not account for the role of religion and ethnicity in the development of citizenship, he did stress the difficulties empires faced in developing a loyal population that would oppose various vested interests. He also noted that these empires were forced to embark upon a series of reforms, however shallow, in order to compete in the arena of Great Power politics.

Mann's analysis of citizenship as a "ruling class strategy" imposed on subjects in order to create social integration is an excellent starting point for discussion of the Ottoman conception of citizenship, which was constructed by a centralizing monarchy of the nineteenth century. This was not a citizenship that was initially promulgated by demands from

13. More recently, in the face of unimaginable changes that have occurred since the fall of the Soviet Union and the Warsaw Pact in 1989, the dismantling of authoritarian regimes in Latin America, the end of apartheid in South Africa, and the outbreak of ethnic wars from Eastern Europe to Africa, scholars have been confronted with new paradigms by which to understand the rise of ethnic nationalisms at the time that larger territorial units such as the European Union seek to create a citizenship based on loyalty to multiethnic, corporate entities. In contrast to earlier discussions of citizenship which were connected to the nation-state, in the 1990s scholars began to examine how citizenship might become internationalized along the lines of Immanuel Kant's vision of a "world civil society" (see Van Steenbergen 1994, 6–7). Jürgen Habermas considered the issue of a European citizenship that transcends national borders (see Habermas 1994, 20–35). Richard Falk proposed that there was a natural process that leads from the city-state to the nation-state and regional corporate identities, to, finally, a global citizenship (see Falk 1994, 127–40).

Ottoman subjects for rights. To the contrary, the ruling elites extended certain privileges to the population in order to strengthen the empire and centralize control over the peripheries (Mann 1987, 339–54).[14]

The classical Ottoman system of state included only two classes: the *askeri,* who ruled the empire, and the *reaya,* who had certain compulsory obligations to the state such as paying taxes and performing military service. In performing these duties, the citizen acknowledged his or her acceptance of the political and social order imposed by the state. A citizen who was loyal to the state would also benefit from economic prosperity and political and social stability.

The Ottomans enacted three important decrees that established the basis for imperial citizenship. The Nobel Rescript of the Rose Garden *(Hatt-ı Şerif-i Gülhane)* of 3 November 1839 ushered in the Tanzimat period and was the framework of all future reforms and legislation. While upholding the primacy of Shari'a law, the Rescript declared the equality of all peoples in the empire without regard to their faith and with no distinction on the basis of communal affiliations:

> The Muslim and non-Muslim subjects of our lofty Sultanate shall, without exception, enjoy our imperial concessions. Therefore we grant perfect security to all the populations of our Empire in their lives, their honor, and their properties according to the sacred law.[15]

The Rescript was an attempt to impose legal equality and universal obligations on the diverse religious and ethnic communities in the empire. The main provisions of the Rescript included abolishing tax farming and regularizing military conscription for Muslim males. It emphasized the rights of the individual (male) subject over the former privileges of corporate bodies such as guilds, tribes, and other military and civil associations.

The Reform Rescript of 1856 *(Islahat Fermanı)* reasserted and reaffirmed the rights of all subjects to freedom of religion. This restatement of the 1839 Rescript was an attempt to stem the tide of nationalist fervor

14. See also Arat 2000, 275.

15. See Hurewitz 1974, 269–71, for a translation of the *Hatt-ı Şerif-i Gülhane.*

in the Balkans, and to prevent French and Russian intrigue among Catholic and Orthodox communities. The Rescript removed the *dhimmi* status of non-Muslims by abolishing the discriminatory poll tax *(cizye)* and allowing non-Muslims the right to be educated in state schools and employed in the bureaucracy. In line with Mann's observations, these rescripts represented the ruling class's bestowal of rights upon its subjects in order to lessen the power of vested interests that were resistant to Ottoman policies of centralization (Salzmann 1999, 41–42; Arat 2000, 276; Akiba 2007, 45–46).

By the 1860s, official imperial nationalism, Ottomanism, with its vision of a multiethnic and multireligious empire whose subjects were primarily loyal to the dynasty, upheld the hierarchical ruling-class structure of the sultanate and the people. Reflecting on Ottomanism and citizenship after the 1861 massacres in Mount Lebanon and Damascus, Fuad Paşa, the Ottoman foreign minister, declared that subject-citizens were required to maintain an uncritical loyalty to the sultan, who embodied the nation and who maintained stability but also treated each subject with compassion and justice. Fuad Paşa described his conception of common citizenship *(hemşirilik)* as an "empty vessel to be filled by the center, to be disciplined and then reformed by the authoritarian but benevolent and modernizing power of the imperial state" (Makdisi 2002a, 606–8). A contrary vision of citizenship was put forth by Butrus al-Bustani, a Syrian intellectual who promoted his views in a series of pamphlets he wrote about the 1860 massacres. Al-Bustani called for a secular citizenship that included an identity that transcended religious affiliations. He did not agree with the top-down approach of Fuad Paşa, and instead called for equal relations between the government and its citizens, and between the center and its peripheries. Al-Bustani's hypothetical citizens were informed, educated, and actively involved in the affairs of the empire. Where Fuad Paşa believed it was the right of the government to mold its subjects into citizens, al-Bustani asserted that it was the responsibility of the subjects to make themselves into citizens. Fuad Paşa's views represented official imperial nationalism, while al-Bustani's conceived of a nation where individuals had a local identification within the broader imperial framework (Makdisi 2002a, 608).

The most definitive statement of Ottoman nationality and the relationship of the ruler to his subjects, as well the clearest declaration about who would be included in Ottoman citizenship, was the Law of Ottoman Nationality *(Tabi'iyet-i Osmaniye Kanunnamesi),* enacted 19 January 1869.[16] The nationality law was one of a number of laws and decrees promulgated during the Tanzimat era as a part of Ottoman centralizing policies that attempted to bring persons, as well as the peripheral territories and their resources, under central management. The law outlined basic rights and created a political identity based on birth or residence [*jus sanguinis* and *jus soli*], thereby allowing the government to designate who were legal residents and who were foreigners (Saltzmann 1999, 45). Article 1 stated, "Persons born at the time when their parents or only [their] father are of Ottoman nationality are considered Ottoman subjects." This was a declaration of *jus sanguinis* through the paternal line. Articles 2 and 3 were pronouncements of the right of citizenship through residence, *jus soli.* In Article 2, persons born in the Ottoman Empire whose parents were foreign nationals could claim Ottoman citizenship within three years after reaching the age of majority. In Article 3, a foreigner who had lived in the Ottoman Empire for five consecutive years could petition for Ottoman citizenship (Unat 1966, 8–9).[17]

It is impossible to determine the intention of the framers of this law with respect to the practical effects of citizenship on the rights and responsibilities of the state to its subjects, and the subjects to the state. This term, *tebaa,* was ambiguous and could mean both "subject" and "citizen." In Ottoman legal documents, during the last fifty years of the empire, the term was often used interchangeably with the French *citoyen.* Such interchangeability of terminology in legal documents suggests that judicial reformers easily utilized new terminology as needed and may not have necessarily intended to promote a profound shift from subject status to citizenship, and a concurrent change in the relationship that shift would imply between the ruler and his subjects.

16. See appendix B.

17. *Düstur,* 1. tertip, 1. cilt, s. 16–18. A translation of the Ottoman nationality law can be found in Flournoy and Hudson 1929, 568.

In the course of this study, we will examine subsequent legislation and government policies in order to analyze the meaning of "citizen" *(tebaa),* and its practical ramifications. In terms of the practical ramifications of the rights and responsibilities of citizens, two areas of legislation will be considered—the requirement for military service and the right to own property and inherit and dispose of the estates of the deceased—both of which were essential for control of the Ottoman provinces of Iraq.

Sultan Abdülhamid II continued the Tanzimat Reforms, especially the administrative changes put into effect in the previous four decades, which had become a permanent part of the political landscape. His vision was an authoritarian one, however, and there was little possibility of a transparent relationship between the sultan and his subjects that would create a more open process of political participation. The sultan did recognize the need for continuing the process of centralization, especially in peripheral regions. Abdülhamid was concerned with increasing the effectiveness of his military, particularly because the empire had experienced significant territorial losses. Effective universal conscription was essential to the success of this program.

Universal conscription had long been a goal of nineteenth-century sultans. Mahmud II (1808–1839), for example, recognized the need for a more professional army after being defeated by Mehmed 'Ali's conscripts in Syria in the early 1830s. The Noble Rescript of the Rose Garden of 1839 also noted that the application of a more equitable conscription system was necessary for all subjects of the empire. The Prussian model of conscription for universal military service was introduced in 1844, with detailed regulations set forth in the Regulation for Military Conscription *(Kur'a Nizamnamesi)* of 1848. This law remained the model until new regulations were enacted in 1869 that outlined a tiered system of service, including active duty, reserve units, and, finally, guards who were not expected to serve on active duty. This tiered system was codified in a new law, the *Kur'a Nizamnamesi* of 1871 and remained in force until the Constitutional Revolution of 1908. In 1886, the Ottomans instituted a series of reforms known as the Recruitment Regulation *(Ahz-ı Asker Nizamnamesi)* that strengthened bureaucratic control over the conscription process. These reforms were enacted at a time when expansion of the armed forces had become imperative as a result of the Ottoman defeat in the Ottoman-Russian War of 1877 to 1878.

The second area of concern for citizens that saw significant legislation was land reform. Land reforms throughout the nineteenth century illustrated the difficulties faced by the Ottoman government as it attempted to transform freehold *(mülk)* landowners, who had the right to tax revenues, to single-title property holders, which would allow for an individual taxation system. Land reforms were also a part of the centralization process that was meant to ensure state control over resources through the regularization of land registration, cadastral surveys and mapping, and taxation. The earliest pronouncements of land reform in the nineteenth century were again seen in the 1839 Noble Rescript of the Rose Garden, which insured the security of property, life, and honor for Ottoman subjects. The decree affirmed the right of subjects to possession *(tasarruf)* and ownership *(malik)* of movable *(emval)* and immovable *(emlak)* properties (İslamoğlu 2000, 7–8, 40). Fundamentally the decree sought to reign in vested interests in the tax farming system, and instead shift the creation of wealth to farmers, artisans, and traders. Administrative departments were created to see to the expansion of this wealth (Mundy and Smith 2007, 40–45). A series of decrees (included in the *Mesail-i Mühimme İradeleri*) in the 1840s created the infrastructure to regulate taxation, and supported a more equitable system through the collection of information on the needs of agriculturalists. Registration of the individual estates of artisans, traders, the religious class, and family farms was undertaken for taxation purposes initially in Anatolia and Rumeli, but not in the Arab provinces, which lacked the infrastructure necessary to carry out the registration. These reforms established the principle of a property tax that linked the registration of taxable property to the individual—the individuation of tax responsibility. The *Ahkam-ı Meriye* of 1849 continued the fundamental succession rights of agricultural land to sons, and extended the right to inherit land from fathers and mothers to daughters as well. Daughters previously had not been considered cultivators and were excluded under administrative law from succession rights. But daughters were now counted as part of the agricultural family and were given the right to inheritance. It is important to emphasize that the

Ahkam-ı Meriye was administrative law *(kanun)* related to agricultural land and not to urban land. This was separate from the Shari'a, which had always given daughters the right to inherit. The fact that this administrative law sought to remedy an injustice to daughters by allowing them inheritance rights in the agricultural sphere supports the contention of most scholars that nineteenth-century jurists were formulating laws by drawing from the arenas of both administrative and religious law in order to find interpretations relevant to the exigencies of the empire. In other words, there was an overlapping of administrative and Islamic jurisprudence (İslamoğlu 2000, 10–11; Mundy and Smith 2007, 40–45).

The Land Code of 1858 *(Kanun-ı Arazi),* the Cadastral Regulation of 1859 *(Tapu Nizamnamesi),* and the Provincial Laws of 1864 and 1871 introduced further important changes in land legislation. The provisions of the Land Code and the Cadastral Regulation related to landed property and did not deal with taxation, which was covered under other legislation. In line with general centralization policies, the Code regulated all forms of landed wealth as a means to extract the greatest revenue. The Code allowed title owners to claim exclusive ownership over state *(miri)* land. Ownership in the Ottoman context of the mid–nineteenth century did not mean an absolute right, but rather a claim to production and land revenues. These regulations effectuated state control over all aspects of land transactions, including registration and leasing procedures, as well as over other transactions, such as the right of irrevocable transfer *(ferağ)* and protection against confiscation for indebtedness (İslamoğlu 2000, 26–31).

Provincial laws of 1864 and 1871 established local councils on the village level, and provincial departments of finance, correspondence, agriculture, commerce, education, roads, pious foundations, and policing. The responsibilities of these departments included the administration of property, registration, and taxation. Property law expanded in the 1870s to include mortgages and foreclosures, and also established a definition for "immoveable property" *(emval-i gayr-i menkule)* that included freehold *(mülk),* foundation *(vakıf),* and state *(miri)* lands. Where previously the individual was responsible for obtaining title *(tapu)* documents, in 1871, survey teams were being sent out in an additional effort to ensure the registration of all land (Mundy and Smith 2007, 45–52).[18] The success of the Tanzimat military and land reforms was evident wherever the Ottomans exercised direct rule. It proved more difficult to impose the reforms in areas outside of the provincial centers and in frontier regions, which were still ruled by local interests.

The Ottoman Imperial Enterprise and the Iraqi Frontier

Scholars of Ottoman history have only just begun to produce important studies on Ottoman imperialism and centralizing policies—both of which attempted to extend the sultan's authority to the frontier regions. Homi Bhabha and Selim Deringil have suggested that scholars of colonialism and postcolonialism have ignored the Ottoman experience with imperialism because it is somehow slightly different from the European version. (Bhabha 1994, 85–92; Deringil 2003, 313–14). The Ottomans were a Muslim power that fell outside standard discussions of imperialism as a European phenomenon. Ussama Makdisi maintains further that Ottoman historians' focus on deconstructing the "decline" theory has produced many studies emphasizing the complexity of interpreting the eighteenth century's influence on the modernizing efforts of the nineteenth, but has also led to their neglecting Ottoman imperialism (2002b, 29–48).

Irrespective of the newness of this field in Ottoman studies, historians are increasingly making important connections between Ottoman imperialism, its centralizing policies, and its borderland regions. Ottoman imperial policies in the nineteenth century were based on a centralization program that aimed to revive and strengthen the empire. They were put in place in response to European encroachments and in recognition that the empire's territorial integrity was in danger. These policies were fundamentally a "civilizing mission" over peripheral regions that reformers considered primitive and savage—areas rife with fanaticism, ignorance,

18. The former categories of land remained until quite late in the empire—until 1912—when laws were issued that established a uniform category of land "modeled" on those of European nations. Although the 1912 laws were not implemented in the Arab provinces—these territories had devolved from the empire before the laws could be enacted—the laws became a legacy to the British and French legal systems in the Mandate period.

and sectarianism. Border regions were places of "danger and anxiety" and in need of reform in order to ensure the stability of the state (Makdisi 2002b, 29–32; Deringil 2003, 311–42).[19]

Eugene Rogan has presented an excellent working definition for the Ottoman "frontiers." They were areas that encompassed "socio-political orders apart from the institutions of the Empire at large" (1999, 6). On the frontiers, there was interaction between ethnically, culturally, and religiously distinct societies, and these indigenous societies clashed with outsiders who imposed their policies upon the region. Frontier regions included cities, towns, villages, and tribes that had their own institutions of governance and policing, and possessed their own military capacities that resisted the empire's centralizing policies. If these regions were not brought under the authority of the centralizing empire, then they potentially might come under control of other near neighbors or lean toward their own independence. The three Ottoman provinces of Basra, Baghdad, and Mosul was a frontier region of cities, towns, and villages, as well as tribal populations that were resistant to conquest and settlement. Control of the provinces was difficult because of their distance from the center of power and because of the role they played as a backdrop to the Sunni-Shi'i conflict. The frontier region was contested by the Iranians, whose interest centered on the four shrine cities of Najaf, Karbala', Kadhimiyya, and Samarra', all of which were sites of early Shi'i history and sacred to Shi'i Islam. This zone was marked throughout the period of empires by an Ottoman-Iranian contest for political, religious, social, and economic control.[20]

Recent examinations of the Ottoman frontiers in the nineteenth century have highlighted Ottoman concerns over controlling borders during a period of territorial losses because of internal independence movements and encroachments from the West (Rogan 1996, 1999; Najmabadi 1998; Kühn 2002, 2003a; Blumi 2003a and 2003b; Deringil 2003). These

19. On the question of the border as a region of danger and anxiety, see Najmabadi 1998.

20. This conflict began in the early sixteenth century with the rise of the Safavid state and two periods of Safavid occupation of Baghdad, from 1508 to 1533 and from 1622 to 1638 (see Nakash 1994, 14–17; Peirce 2003, 24–25, 253–58).

studies have noted the various ways the Ottoman government's centralization program sought to exert tighter controls over the borderlands by introducing new administrative units, more efficient methods of tax collection, educational institutions, customs houses, railroads, and other forms of cultural and economic penetration.[21] None of these studies, however, has examined the linkages between the construction of citizenship, gender, and religious conversion to Ottoman policies that sought to bring centralized control to the Iraqi frontier provinces. The primary focus of this book is an analysis of these linkages in the final half-century of the empire in the frontier provinces of Iraq. The specific vehicle of this analysis will be the only exclusion made to the Law of Ottoman Nationality of 1869: the prohibition of marriages between Ottoman women and Iranian men. It is hoped, ultimately, that this study will contribute to the evolving discussion of the complex relationship of the Ottoman central government with its peripheries, and introduce the gender equation into this conversation.

The Demographic Importance of Marriage and the Politics of Reproduction

Recent examinations of the frontier provinces of the Ottoman Empire have had little to say about the relationship between Ottoman centralizing institutions, the construction of citizenship, and the demographic importance of marriage. Marriage, demographically, had a variety of social and economic effects on the fabric of society and reached into the very heart of public order and moral behavior. The Ottomans determined that control of marriage in their easternmost border territories was an essential element in their control of this peripheral region.[22]

21. There were, of course, earlier works that referred to the importance of examining the Ottoman borders. To mention just a few examples, see Lewis 1955, Mardin 1973, and Akarlı 1990.

22. For a discussion of the demographic impact of marriage on society see Anne-Lise Head-König 1993. Head-König considered religious and secular legal restraints on the rights of adults to contract marriages in the Catholic and Protestant cantons of Switzerland. She discussed marriages that were not acceptable to the society, and how they

Definitions of citizenship for most countries in the nineteenth century was intimately linked with the institution of marriage and the relationship between husband and wife—the wife being the subordinate member and the husband having the personal power as head of the household. As a result of this relationship, the husband carried the status of "citizen" (Flournoy and Hudson 1929). As Ursula Vogel has demonstrated in her examination of the gender component of citizenship, this model worked to create a perceived stability, not only in the marital structure but also within the broader society of the state. In order for the husband to carry the status of citizenship, he had to maintain the personal power of head of the household, a formulation that did not contradict nineteenth-century notions of familial relations in most countries. The husband's control of the family, for example, assured control over the sexuality of his wife and the legitimacy of his offspring. In the broader society, a woman's inferior status within her marriage gave her no choice in terms of citizenship. Her role was to maintain communal stability—politically and morally—because female domestic virtue created public virtue. While carrying out her duties, the wife supported her husband in his obligation to the community and instilled in her children loyalty to the state (Vogel 1991, 67–75; Walby 1992, 82–87, and 1994, 370–81; Orloff 1993, 308–9; Judson 1996, 5). Floya Anthias and Nira Yuval-Davis show five areas in which women's status is connected to nationalism and citizenship:

1. Women biologically produce within their ethnic group, and government policies may seek to increase or limit the number of children born within specific ethnic communities in order to maintain a desired ethnic dominance within the state.

2. Women's biological reproduction maintains the boundaries of their ethnic group from generation to generation. They must contract a legal marriage, within religious and social traditions, so that offspring may be considered legitimate members of the community.

---

could influence, socially and economically, the fabric of that society. I wish to thank Nicole van Os for bringing this article to my attention.

> 3. Women are the ideological and cultural carriers and teachers of the traditions and heritage of their community.
>
> 4. Women are often the loved symbol of the nation. In nationalist discourse, men defend the honor of their wives and children.
>
> 5. Women participate in the national struggles of their nation in varying degrees, but generally as supporters and nurturers of males who do the fighting. (1989, 6–15)

Anthias and Yuval-Davis emphasized that the historical experiences connecting women's status to the state varied greatly from country to country and over the centuries. Some states interfered in women's biological rights through the legislative process, whereas in other countries the state left such "private" matters to individual choice. They also noted that women often accepted these roles and even participated in the process (1989, 10–11). In the case of the law prohibiting Ottoman women from marrying Iranian men, the government was clearly attempting to control women's biological choices by limiting the number of children who would be considered Iranian citizens. The government was relegating its women to the roles as symbols of the nation, or markers of boundaries and models of difference.

Married women's basic citizenship rights were derived from the Code Napoléon of 1804, which was the legal model that influenced many parts of the world, including the Ottoman Empire, with respect to both its own reforms in the legal arena and to its conception of citizenship. Concerning marriage, the Code upheld the pre-Revolutionary view of the importance of protecting the husband's position as the head of the household. This model was challenged in France at the end of the nineteenth century when women began to gain control over property—a basic requirement for citizenship that would eventually lead to their achieving the status of full citizens. But the position of the husband as head of the family was not challenged at this point. With respect to the demographic importance of marriage and the construction of citizenship, for most of the nineteenth century the institution of marriage was the primary obstacle to women attaining choice in citizenship rights (Vogel 1991, 75–79). It is important to note that under Islamic law women could own property. The French code, therefore, did not effect any change in Muslim lands where, because of ease of divorce, property did not merge upon marriage. This was a more important issue in Christian and Jewish societies where women brought property to their marriages. In this case, French law, which is often assumed to be more progressive than Islamic law, was not an innovation, because Muslim women could own property.

In most countries in the late nineteenth century, the politics of marriage were also intimately connected to the formation of nationalism and the nation-state. Women's subordinate position within marriage, and their lack of choice of citizenship, was utilized for domestic and geopolitical exigencies. The connection between women and the state is a large and complex subject that is evidenced by the vast body of literature produced in the past thirty years.[23] Although few studies have been produced concerning the connection between women and nationalism in the Ottoman Empire, a number of factors can be extrapolated from this vast body of literature to the specific historical experience of the relationship between Ottoman centralizing policies in the Iraqi provinces and the government's position on the status of women within those policies. Primary to Ottoman interests in securing the three eastern provinces of Baghdad, Basra, and Mosul was its concern with the differences in religion (Sunni or Shi'i) and ethnicity (Ottoman, Iranian, Kurdish) of the population. Concomitant with Ottoman intentions to secure its eastern borders was the need to create and maintain that population's loyalty to the state. The demographic aspect of marriage was important to Ottoman frontier policies because women and their choice of husbands were intimately linked to Ottoman domestic and geopolitical policies. First, with respect specifically to the eastern provinces, women were considered the "biological reproducers" of the society, and Ottoman policies attempted to control the reproductive choices of their female citizens. Female bodies were legally coopted by government control over marriage partners, which was intended to limit the number of

23. For an excellent examination of the connection between women and nationalism in the larger Muslim world, see Rubin 2005.

undesirables (Shi'ites). Second, women were the markers of the boundaries of ethnic, religious, and national groups. The Ottomans' legislation, which was targeted primarily toward its eastern provinces, placed women in the position of maintaining religious, ethnic, and social norms appropriate to the Ottoman-Sunni state. Third, women were considered symbols of the nation and Ottoman cultural identity. Women reinforced Ottoman culture by passing on the language, rituals, and myths of the culture to their children. Fourth, women were models of difference, at the center of ethnic, religious, and national identity struggles between the Ottomans and Iranians over control of the territory in the Iraqi provinces. Women, in their choice of marriage partners, were participants in the national, economic, political, and military struggles between the Ottomans and Iranians in the Ottoman eastern provinces. All of these factors highlight how the Ottoman policy to control women's choice of marriage partners was particularly important in the frontier regions where women (and the nation) needed to be protected against invasion and any violation of its boundaries.[24]

From the late nineteenth to the early twentieth centuries, Muslim and non-Muslim officials from the respective religious communities controlled the performance of marriage and related issues of personal status, such as divorce, inheritance, and child custody. After the enactment of the Law of Ottoman Nationality in 1869, the state had a greater opportunity to interfere in personal status issues where they concerned imperial authority and territorial hegemony. This opportunity was particularly evident in the government's control of the rights and obligations of citizenship, such as conscription, taxation, and matters of inheritance that, in practice, had never been the exclusive domain of religious authority.[25]

24. These categories were first defined by Floya Anthias and Nira Yuval-Davis (1989, 7). Their work was later expanded upon by Walby (1992, 81–99) and Peterson (1994, 77–83). For an excellent discussion of gender fear and the borders of the nation, see Najmabadi 1998. For a recent compilation of articles about broader historical and contemporary issues concerning gender, citizenship, and the Middle East, see Joseph 2000.

25. In classical Islamic law, marriages were restricted to a greater degree for Muslim women than for Muslim men. A man could marry a Muslim woman or a woman

As the Ottomans adopted the concept of citizenship from European legal systems, they also modified its definition to conform to their particular geopolitical concerns in the eastern frontier provinces. The Ottomans made one, and only one, very important exception to the imperial definition of citizenship as enacted in the Law of Ottoman Nationality of 1869. In 1874, responding to reports of large-scale conversion of the Iraqi population from Sunni to Shiʿi Islam, the Ottomans enacted a law prohibiting marriages between Ottoman women and Iranian men.

The 1874 law demonstrates the demographic importance of marriage for Ottoman centralizing policies in the frontier provinces of Iraq. Ottoman attempts to bring the provinces under the control of the central administration were directly connected to geopolitical realities that centered on the centuries-long rivalry between Ottoman and Iranian leaders, which often took the form of Sunni-Shiʿi hostility. In the construction of citizenship in the mid–nineteenth century, the Ottomans took into account both historical and contemporary geopolitical exigencies, and they legislated citizenship rights to reflect these realities. Officials had the perception that Shiʿism was increasing among the population and seriously threatening the government's control over the provinces. The 1874 prohibition would aid in maintaining the loyalty of the population, decrease the number of soldiers in the Sixth Army who were suspected of being Shiʿa, and also prevent the material wealth of the empire from falling into the hands of Iranian citizens. The main focus of this book is, therefore, an examination of the marriage prohibition as part of the process of extending the Empire's centralizing policies to the Iraqi frontier provinces, where reports of conversions took on special importance within the broad range of geopolitical concerns over control of the provinces.

---

from among the "Peoples of the Book," but a Muslim woman could only marry another Muslim or a convert to Islam. Peoples of the Book included persons whose religions had revealed texts. Jews, Christians, Zoroastrians, Sabeans, and Hindus were included in this category. Within Islam, additionally, there was no legal restriction on Sunni-Shiʿi marriage, although social pressure may certainly have been an obstacle to such unions.

The Structure of the Book

This book is divided into six chapters. Chapter 1 provides the historical background to the Sunni-Shi'i conflict beginning in the sixteenth century with the establishment of the Safavid-Shi'ite Empire in 1501. It also contains a discussion of Ottoman *fetva* literature, which designated the Safavids as dangerous heretics and prohibited marriages between Sunnis and Shi'ites. This discussion is essential to understanding the rhetorical foundation of nineteenth-century laws prohibiting these marriages. The framers of the nineteenth-century marriage prohibitions consistently reached back to "ancient times" to lend the prohibition authority and legitimacy. This chapter ends with the first restatement of the prohibition of marriage in the nineteenth century, the *Buyruldu-ı 'Ali* of 1822, an imperial decree of Mahmud II, which carried on the age-old discourse of heresy at a time of increased tension between the two empires. The sultan's decision to restate the prohibition, at this time, highlights the importance of geopolitical factors in the Iraqi provinces. The entire discussion in chapter 1 is about various *fetvas,* decrees, instructions, and regulations and is not concerned with how officials implemented these decrees. It is clear what was intended by these decrees, but it was not clear from the archival sources and secondary literature how these decrees were enforced. Archival documents from the latter half of the nineteenth century contain more detail on the government's rulings in specific cases, and the mechanisms for enforcing the marriage prohibition. The means of enforcement of the laws are discussed in chapters 3 and 4.

Chapter 2 examines the most important concern for the Ottomans in controlling the Iraqi border provinces during the nineteenth century—the activities of Shi'i *ulema* in converting the Sunni population to Shi'ism. In discussions in various ministries and in the Cabinet, the increase of the Shi'i population was consistently highlighted as one of the reasons for continuing the ban on marriages between Ottomans and Iranians. Various reports in archival documents illuminate Ottoman worries over this increase and their attempts to halt Shi'i missionary activity.

The first two chapters deal with the historical background to Ottoman concerns over control of the Iraqi provinces, Ottoman centralizing policies, and Ottoman recognition of the demographic importance of marriage in controlling the frontier regions. These chapters lead into the discussion of the construction of Ottoman citizenship. Chapter 3 introduces the process through which the Ottomans adopted and adapted their citizenship law—the Law of Ottoman Nationality of 1869, to geopolitical necessities. In this case, the Ottomans made their only exception to nationality law when, in 1874, they enacted the law prohibiting marriage between Ottoman women and Iranian men. The importance of the singular exclusion of Ottoman women from marrying Iranian men is emphasized by examining two other case studies that came to the attention of the Cabinet and legal advisors—the legality of marriages between Ottoman women and Algerian men, who held French citizenship, and between Ottoman women and Greek men, who held Greek citizenship. In considering these other cases, the Ottomans showed the legal rationale by which they adapted the Ottoman nationality law to serve the geopolitical needs of empire where they were considered most critical—on its eastern frontier. This chapter also discusses the mechanisms established for enforcing the prohibition of marriage, which sanctioned officials and guardians who allowed these marriages. The Ottoman administration intended these laws and procedures to add clarity and finality to the question of marriage between Ottoman women and Iranian men, but in examining various case studies it is clear that confusion remained among provincial officials over who was included in the prohibition and over the procedures for its enforcement.

Key to the prohibition of marriages were the rights and responsibilities of citizenship, and the impact of those responsibilities on Ottoman control of the Iraqi provinces. Chapter 4 highlights two rights and responsibilities that were of particular importance. The first responsibility was to perform military service. The government was keenly diligent to ensure that all men would be registered and would serve as loyal soldiers. The second issue was the right to inheritance for both males and females, which had special importance in control over the eastern provinces. Officials were concerned about the transfer of wealth and property into the hands of foreign residents. Both of these matters were the main concerns for official in the Iraqi provinces, where the majority of the population was Shiʿite and many residents held Iranian citizenship.

Chapter 5 examines the prohibition of marriages between Ottoman women and Iranian men in the post-Hamidian period when earlier concerns about Iranian influence in the eastern provinces gave way to different geopolitical realities, such as increasing British and Russian interests in the region. The prohibition was continually challenged both by the Iranian government and by various Ottoman ministries and legal advisors. They all questioned the need to continue the prohibition during a world war and after the loss of the Iraqi provinces at the end of hostilities. This chapter highlights these discussions and debates, and ends with a discussion of the cancellation of the prohibition in 1926, which occurred along with the revision of the legal system under the administration of the Republic of Turkey.

1

The Historical Background of the Sunni-Shi'i Conflict

Classical Theory of the State in Islam and the Problem of Inter-Muslim Territorial Division

The Ottomans emerged and consolidated their empire from the thirteenth to the fifteenth centuries—a period when regional Muslim dynasties were the norm. In the thirteenth century, the Mongols overran Baghdad and conquered much of western Asia. In Egypt, the Mamluk sultanate—Turkic slave soldiers—seized power from the Ayyubid dynasty (1169–1250) and would rule until 1517. Other regional Muslim empires such as the Delhi sultanates (1206–1526) and the Timurid Mughal Empire (1370–1526) existed near the Ottoman geopolitical environment. The Safavids emerged in the thirteenth century as a mystical movement around Ardabil on the borders of modern Iran and Azerbaijan. By the fifteenth century, the Safavids had transformed themselves into a messianic militant movement, which preached armed struggle against other Muslim regimes that they perceived as transgressing the boundaries of Islam. Under Shah Isma'il (1487–1524) the Shi'i-Safavid Empire (1501–1722) occupied Tabriz and within a decade completed their conquest of Iran.

Ottoman officials surely must have considered how to define the political, economic, and legal obligations that would arise among separate Muslim empires. In the formative years of Islam, jurists who pondered political theories concerning the ideal Islamic state and the practice of governance worked during a time of a weakened central administration located in Baghdad. During this period, the greater Muslim community *(umma)* had been politically divided as a consequence of semi-independent dynastic regimes that ruled in the far-flung provinces.

Spain, for example, had come under the control of the Umayyads; Tunisia under the Aghlabids; and Egypt and Syria under the Fatimids, the Ayyubids, and later the Mamluks. Jurists recognized territorial pluralism and accorded the caliph in Baghdad the role of defender of the community and protector of Muslim lands. Al-Mawardi (d. 1058) served as a Shafi'i judge *(qadi)* in a number of Iraqi districts, including Baghdad. He wrote a seminal work on Islamic state theory at a time when the central 'Abbasid caliphate was no longer the possessor of unified caliphal authority, was under direct threat from the Shi'i-Fatimids in Egypt, and was subject to Shi'i-Buyid amirs in Baghdad (Khadduri 1955, 12, 142; Rosenthal 1958, 27–37; Lambton 1981, 90; Donner 1986, 295). In an effort to protect and strengthen the institution of the caliphate, al-Mawardi rejected the possibility of two or more rulers *(imams)* and held that in an ideal state there should be only one ruler of the Muslim community *(dar al-Islam)*. Other jurists, who more directly reflected upon the political realities, disagreed with al-Mawardi on this question. Al-Baghdadi (d. 1037), an Ash'ari and contemporary of al-Mawardi, recognized the geopolitical realities of his time. He concluded that two rulers could be in power and enforce the law in their own realms, but only if their domains were far apart and separated by sea so that they could not wage war against one another (Lambton 1981, 78–79). This thesis legitimized Umayyad control of Spain, which was not a direct threat to the central institutions of the state in Baghdad. It was, however, aimed more directly at the Fatimid challenge in Egypt, delegitimizing this immediate and serious worry of the central administration.

In the ensuing centuries, theorists were concerned, not so much with the problem of having more than one caliph, but with finding a solution to the fragmentation of territory by military commanders and local chieftains. Al-Ghazali (d. 1111) wrote at a time when the caliphate was no longer the central political institution, and he spoke directly about the problem of dual authority, specifically the moral leadership of the caliph and the military power of the amirs (Rosenthal 1958, 38–43; Lambton 1981, 112). In seeking to understand the balance of power between these forces and in aiming to avoid civil chaos *(fitna)*, al-Ghazali maintained that the caliphate belonged to the 'Abbasids, who protected the religious and cultural unity of Islam. But the amirs, who were central to the functioning of the state, could hold real power if they accepted the authority of the caliph by swearing allegiance to him, ensured that the caliph was mentioned in the Friday prayers, and recorded his name on all coinage. For al-Ghazali, it was better to accept the political realities and ensure political stability than to have the community subjected to civil strife. It is important to note that al-Ghazali's position was taken during a period when there was a resurgence of Sunni orthodoxy after the fall of the Shi'i-Buyids. His view reasserted the supremacy of the caliph as the head of the *umma* while finding a place for the amirates within the government structure. After the fall of the 'Abbasid caliphate in 1258, however, with few exceptions, jurists ceased their discussion of the caliphate as a central institution—religious, cultural or political. The Mongol invasions finally put an end to the myth of a universal caliphate.[1]

Ibn Taymiyya (d. 1328), a Hanbali jurist, found a solution to the problem of Muslim unity in the absence of a central caliphate by declaring that religious unity was the overriding factor in maintaining the aggregate in a politically divided territory. Sovereignty was no longer in the hands of one imam, but was held by a scholar like himself whose learning and virtue required him to interpret the law and apply it to changing circumstances (Rosenthal 1958, 51–61; Lambton 1981, 146; Piscatori 1986, 47). These scholars would unify Muslims by keeping alive the Shari'a as the foundation of the state.

Ibn Khaldun (d. 1406), the chief judge of the Maliki legal school in Cairo and a famous geographer and sociologist, brought the discussion back to the role of the caliph in Muslim society, but his analysis was based on the particular milieu he worked in—the lands of North Africa, where civil disorders and rapid changes of dynasties were the norm. In line with his most famous theory of the rise and decline of states, he found that territorial divisions were in conformity with Islam. He even went as far as to

1. Ibn Jama'a (d. 1333), a Shafi'i judge, was indeed a voice in the wilderness. He accepted the possibility that less than qualified caliphs could rule, but refused to allow the rule of two imams at the same time (see Lambton 1981, 142).

maintain that competent, even nondynastic leadership was preferable to weak dynastic claims. According to Ibn Khaldun, the caliphate no longer need belong to the *Quraysh* (the family of the Prophet Muhammed), because through corruption and decadence they had shown that they no longer possessed the group feeling *('asabiyya)* required for leadership. Others had long since replaced the *Quraysh* with the requisite spirit to rule (Lambton 1981, 396–401).[2] Ibn Khaldun's work was well known to Ottoman scholars (Fleischer 1983, 198–220).

Before turning to the problem of Ottoman legitimacy, it is worthwhile looking at one last theorist, Fadl Allah b. Ruzbihan Khungi (d. 1521), a Sunni jurist who was writing from Özbek territory at the time of Ottoman expansion and Safavid ascendancy. During his early years, there were no claimants to the caliphate, and it was only at the very end of his life that the Ottoman sultan Selim I laid claim to the caliphal title. Fadl Allah followed the long tradition of Sunni state theory by declaring that the role of the caliph was as defender of Islamic lands and protector of the Shari'a. Although ideally the caliph should be from the family of the *Quraysh,* Fadl Allah was speaking to the powers of the day when he maintained that, if there was no *Quraysh* with the qualifications, then a non-Arab *('ajam),* even a Turk, could be appointed to the position. Being aware of the shifting political winds of his time, he allowed an imamate both by nomination and by military force. Fadl Allah was living in a land caught between two warring states—the Ottomans and Safavids—and was residing in a Sunni state that had recently been established by military force. He may well have been aware of Sultan Selim I's claim to the caliphate, and he most certainly knew that military force had recently established both the Safavid state and his own khanate. Geopolitical circumstances, therefore, required that he not hold to the classical theory of a singular caliphate.[3]

2. See also Rosenthal 1958, 84–112; Piscatori 1986, 47.

3. Lambton 1981, 182–85, citing Fadl Allah b. Ruzbihan Khungi's *Suluk al-muluk*, written in 1514 for 'Ubayd Allah, the Özbek khan of Bukhara. Lambton argues that Fadl Allah's lack of insistence on having just one imam was because of the fact that there were none at the time. Yet this ignores the fact that he was well traveled and may certainly have known about the Ottoman sultan's recent claims to the title of caliph.

All of these theories have one problem: they do not discuss the practical problems of inter-Muslim state relations. The Muslim jurists did not outline the legal obligations between two rulers, or the mechanisms necessary to establish working relationships on the political and economic levels. This was to be the Ottoman dilemma when confronted with the establishment of the Safavid state in 1501.

The Ottoman Confrontation with Sectarian Division

The Ottoman Empire encountered the question of the Sunni-Shi'i division as a geopolitical concern with the establishment of the Shi'i-Safavid Empire on its eastern border. A proliferation of Sunni religious opinions *(fetvas)* defined the Shi'a in general, and Shi'i sympathizers *(kızılbaş)* within the Ottoman borders, as heretics. *Kızılbaş* was a term used both derogatorily by Ottoman authorities and with pride by people who expressed loyalty to the Shi'i-Safavi sect *(tarikat)* (Gölpinarlı 1955, 789–95; Watt 1963, 110–21; Mélikoff 1982, 142–54).[4] In the Ottoman Empire, the *kızılbaş* could be found among the Turkmen tribes in the eastern parts of the empire and in the recently acquired border regions of Iraq, where loyalty to the Safavid regime was particularly pronounced.[5] The tribes in these areas had strong theological, ethnic, political, and cul-

---

The fact that he also accused Shah Isma'il and the *kızılbaş* of heresy shows his allegiance to then-current Sunni theories of heresy against the Safavids, and suggests that he could have known and supported the Ottoman claim to sovereignty over the Muslim community.

4. This *tarikat* was founded by Şeyh Safi al-Din (1300–1334). See Walsh 1962, 202–4, for a discussion of the loyalty question. Walsh suggests that the Anatolian tribes were independent of state control and devoted to the interests of the tribes above all else. He also shows how Safavid propaganda in Anatolia was not well organized, and that the local uprisings, prevalent in the area during this period, were the result of initiatives taken by local *şeyhs,* more than any Safavid policy for control of the region.

5. The three provinces bordering on Iran—Basra, Baghdad, and Şehrizol—had previously been ruled by the Safavids and had only come under Ottoman control in 1538. The term *kızılbaş* first appears in the *Mühimme Defterleri* in relation to Iraq in 1577 (see Imber 1979, 248–49).

tural ties to the Safavids. The popularity of *kızılbaş*-ism within the empire became evident in a series of uprisings by tribal leaders in Anatolia. These revolts were clearly an obstacle to Ottoman control and were regarded seriously by Ottoman authorities.

Ottoman religious opinions against the *kızılbaş* evinced growing Ottoman concern about both domestic turmoil and the Safavid challenge to Ottoman hegemony over the greater Muslim community *(umma)* (Peirce 2003, 24–25, 35, 253–58). As a geopolitical matter, the rise of the Shi'i-Safavid state opened a second front that undermined Ottoman foreign policy toward militarily and economically stronger Christian territories in Europe—and the Spanish Empire, in particular, which was an obstacle to Ottoman expansion in North Africa. As a counterbalance to European challenges, the Ottomans established a regional policy based on a unified Muslim state to offset the Christian threat on its western borders. In the early sixteenth century, Sultan Selim I (1512–1520) turned his attention to regional Muslim dynastic states to the south and east. He successfully attacked the Safavids at the Battle of Çaldıran in 1514. He then turned southward, and by 1517 had destroyed the Mamluk sultanate and annexed Egypt, Syria, Palestine, and the holy cities of Mecca and Medina.[6]

As a result of the direct challenge of the Safavids to Ottoman domination of the Islamic world, the sultans in the sixteenth century turned their attention to internal security and became less tolerant of the *kızılbaş* and other heterodox orders in Anatolia. The government began an intentional suppression, which resulted in the deportation and deaths of some 40,000 Safavid sympathizers. This persecution began in preparation for an anticipated battle between Ottoman and Safavid armies at the Battle

6. Walsh 1962, 200–210, offers a very detailed description of the Ottoman campaigns against the Safavids, the repression of tribes in Anatolia, and the polemic against Shi'ism. He claims that these activities were the result of the Ottomans' understanding that the borders of Islam had reached their limits and that the security of the empire now depended on Muslim unity against Christian Europe. It was against this backdrop that the Ottomans sought to strengthen the empire's legitimacy based on the foundations of an "orthodox" Sunni establishment, which took many forms, including opulent displays of spirituality and support for the building of mosques, schools, and hospitals.

of Çaldıran, but the Ottomans continued to pursue the *kızılbaş* movement in eastern Anatolia throughout the sixteenth century (Zarinebaf-Shahr 1997, 1–15).[7] Scholars disagree, however, over the extent to which the Ottomans persecuted their non-*kızılbaş* 'Shi'i' subjects. Devin Stewart noted that Sultan Süleyman I (1520–1566) did order the persecution of individual Shi'i ulema in the Baalbak region of Lebanon (1991, 563–71). But Abdul-Rahim Abu Husayn suggests that, while there may have been individual cases of persecution, there was no Ottoman policy of mass deportations or executions of Ottoman Shi'a, as had been the case with the *kızılbaş* in Anatolia. Incidents of harassment and killing of Ottoman Shi'a were locally motivated and suggested political and religious rivalries more than central policy (1993, 111–13). Marco Salati believes that any distinction in the *fetvas* between Shi'ism and *kızılbaş*-ism had little importance for the Ottoman sultans. Both the Shi'a and *kızılbaş* showed anti-Ottoman tendencies that manifested in a number of ways, including, for example, the cursing of the first three Orthodox caliphs in their mosques (1993, 143–44). Several imperial orders issued concurrently with the establishment of the Safavid state in 1501 are evidence, nevertheless, of a hardening attitude toward Shi'ism by the central Ottoman government (Zarinebaf-Shahr 1997, 6–7). These orders highlight the Ottoman perception that an immediate and severe response was necessary to counterbalance potential threats to the empire from tribes that might sympathize and align themselves with the newly formed Shi'i state. The following imperial order, sent to the governor *(sancakbeyi)* of Sivas in May of 1501, authorized the arrest, punishment, and confiscation of the goods of "Sufis" loyal to Shah Isma'il:

> An imperial order has already been issued to the effect that whoever captures one of the Sufis of Ardabil [the original home territory of the Safavid dynasty], he can seize his goods without being punished. Now,

7. In this article she refers to more than one hundred imperial orders in the *Mühımme Defterleri* sent to local officials instructing them to search out and punish the *kızılbaş*. See also Masters 1991, 4, regarding the events in 1512 when Sultan Selim I arrested Iranian silk merchants in Bursa and had them deported to Istanbul and Rumeli.

> the prince [Selim] has sent his *kul* [servants] and considers fining them the correct punishment. He has ordered me not to interfere in this matter, and has ordered the aforesaid *kul* to fine the Sufis 400 *akçe* each and the *khalifes* [agents of the Shah] 2,000 *akçe* each. I have submitted this petition out of caution. If that is the case, my orders on the Sufi followers of the Ardabiloğlu [followers of Shah Isma'il] are still in effect. Take caution and order your *sipahis* [cavalry soldiers] and men to capture any Sufis on their way to Ardabiloğlu, to strip them and confiscate their goods for themselves. But your *sipahis* should be careful not to use this as a source of income and take their goods away without punishing the captives. It is clear to you how wretched these Sufis are and what calamities they have committed in Iran. You must immediately forbid them to go to Iran. Upon receiving this order, send a report on those who have been captured, and have been stripped so that your rectitude on this matter may become apparent. (Zarinebaf-Shahr 1997, 6–7)

This order, written during the reign of Beyazıd II (1481–1512), refers to Selim (the "prince"), who was to become Selim I. As noted in this order, Prince Selim had imposed fines on those who could not prove their loyalty to the Ottomans. Beyazıd II reaffirmed his order that the *sipahis* could confiscate the property of those "Sufis" who were clearly aligned with the Safavids. Confiscation of property became one of the components of a package of punishments to be levied on supporters of the Safavid Shah.

Prince Selim's interest in this matter at such an early stage was the precursor to a state of affairs that was to consume a major part of his reign. In 1514, during the first major conflict with the Safavids at the Battle of Çaldıran, Sultan Selim I sent the following letter to Shah Isma'il, which outlined both Selim's claim to the caliphate and the Shah's heresy:

> This missive which is stamped with the seal of victory and which is, like inspiration descending from the heavens, witness to the verse "We never chastise until We send forth a Messenger" [Qur'an XVII:15] has been graciously issued by our most glorious majesty—we who are the Caliph of God Most High in this world, far and wide; the proof of

the verse "And what profits men abides in the earth" [Qur'an XIII:17] the Solomon of Splendor, the Alexander of eminence; haloed in victory, Faridun triumphant; slayer of the wicked and the infidel, guardian of the noble and the pious; the warrior in the Path, the defender of the Faith; the champion, the conqueror; the lion, son and grandson of the lion; standard bearer of justice and righteousness, Sultan Selim Shah, son of Sultan Bayezid, son of Sultan Muhammad Khan—and is addressed to the ruler of the kingdom of the Persians, the possessor of the land of tyranny and perversion, the captain of the vicious, the chief of the malicious, the usurping Darius of the time, the malevolent Zahhak of the age, the peer of Cain, Prince Isma'il.

It has been heard repeatedly that you have subjected the upright community of Muhammad (prayers and salutations upon its founder!) to your devious will, that you have undermined the firm foundation of the Faith, that you have unfurled the banner of oppression in the cause of aggression, that you no longer uphold the commandments and prohibitions of the Divine Law, that you have incited your abominable Shi'i faction to unsanctified sexual union and to the shedding of innocent blood, that like they "Who listen to falsehood and consume the unlawful" [Qur'an V:42] you have given ear to idle deceitful words and have eaten that which is forbidden:

He laid waste to mosques, as it is said,
Constructing idol temples in their stead.

That you have rent the noble stuff of Islam with the hand of tyranny, and that you have called the Glorious Qur'an the myths of the Ancients. The rumor of these abominations has caused your name to become like that of Harith deceived by Satan.

Indeed, as both the fatwas of distinguished 'ulema who base their opinion on reason and tradition alike and the consensus of the Sunni community agree that the ancient obligation of expiration, extermination, and expulsion of evil innovation must be the aim of our exalted aspiration, for "Religious zeal is a victory for the Faith of God the Beneficent," then, in accordance with the words of the Prophet (Peace upon him!) "Whosoever introduces evil innovation into our order must be expelled" and "Whosoever does aught against our order must be

> expelled," action has become necessary and exigent. Thus, when the Divine Decree of Eternal Destiny commended the eradication of the infamously wicked infidels into our capable hands, we set out for their lands like ineluctable fate itself to enforce order "Leave not upon the earth of the Unbelievers even one." [Qur'an LXXI:26][8]

This message, which was inspired from the "heavens" and the holy Qur'an, clearly proclaimed the Ottoman Sultan as caliph "far and wide," and compared him to Solomon and Alexander, and other great victorious rulers. The sultan was protector of the faith and the faithful against Shah Isma'il, the promoter of evil. His letter established the right of the Ottoman sultan to leadership of the Muslim community, thereby legalizing Ottoman wars against a Shi'ite state that criminally desecrated the Qur'an, mosques, and other pious institutions, and engaged in sexually immoral behavior. The Shi'a threatened the foundations of the faith (Sunni Islam) by their evil actions, their oppression, and their failure to adhere to the commandments and prohibitions of the religious law. They killed innocent (Sunni) Muslims, destroyed (Sunni) mosques, and built idol temples (Shi'i mosques). They had even gone as far as to deny the authority of the Qur'an and had allowed unlawful sexual unions (most probably a reference to temporary marriage *[mut'a]*). Sultan Selim I was the rightful leader of the community. On the basis of Qur'anic injunctions, the consensus of the Sunni community *(ijma')*, reason *(kiyas)*, and tradition *(sunna)* he was enjoined to expel or exterminate the evil innovation *(bid'a)* of "infamously wicked infidels" that had infiltrated the Sunni order.

This letter detailed accusations of heresy against the Shi'a in general, as well as the Safavids and their supporters in Ottoman territory, that were to become routine in the rhetoric of imperial orders and *fetvas* in the sixteenth century. This language can be analyzed within the context of both Sunni heresiography and the ongoing Ottoman-Safavid conflict. The rise of the Shi'i state challenged the Ottoman's geopolitical status as

8. This English translation of the letter by John E. Woods can be found in McNeill and Waldman 1983, 339–42.

the leader of the Muslim community in a way that other regional Sunni empires could not. The Ottoman struggle with the Safavids was not only based on a struggle for territorial control, but also closely connected to the question of leadership of the Islamic world and the loyalty of both the *kızılbaş* and Ottoman Shiʿa. From the beginning of the establishment of the Shiʿi state, the Ottomans were immersed in a geopolitical struggle whose result was the rhetorical creation of a binary opposition between "true" Islam (Sunni orthodoxy) and Shiʿi "unbelief."

Shah Ismaʿil went to war against the Ottomans and took control of Iraq in 1508. Sunnis in the border regions sought help from the Ottoman sultan to fight against the harsh treatment of the Persians. Although Selim I defeated the Safavids at the Battle of Çaldıran in 1514, this did not put an end to *kızılbaş* disturbances or Safavid interference in Anatolia or Iraq. Nor did the war settle border problems between the two empires. The Safavids reoccupied Iraq for a second time in 1529. Shah Tahmasp I (1533–1576) sent spies and missionaries and used Shiʿite shrines in Iraq as focal points for anti-Sunni, anti-Ottoman activity. The Ottomans, meanwhile, closely inspected dervish orders to search out those who had sympathy with the Safavid state.[9] Süleyman I conducted three campaigns, from 1533 to 1535, in 1548, and from 1553 to 1555, against the Safavids. Finally, in May of 1555, the Ottomans and the Safavids concluded the Amasya Treaty, the first written agreement between the two empires, which allowed the Ottomans to keep their conquests in Iraq and offered mutual recognition, but no lasting peace (Kılıç 2001, 76–78; Finkel 2005, 135).

Sixteenth Century *Fetva* Production and the Prohibition of Marriage

In the period before and immediately following the Battle of Çaldıran, important, anti-Shiʿa *fetvas* emanated from the highest religious officials

9. The Bektaşi and Mevlevi orders were co-opted by offers of land, titles, and honors. Others, such as the Qalandars, Haydaris, Abdals, Jamis, and Shams-i Tabrizis, disappeared from the historical record (see Zarinebaf-Shahr 1997, 8).

in the empire. They were produced in support of government repression of the Shi'a and wars with the Safavid state. The rhetoric of the Ottoman *fetvas* was so forceful that it left no doubt about the official position of "orthodox" Sunni-ism toward the *kızılbaş* and other "heretical" sects, many of whom adhered to the Shi'i school *(mezhep)*. They were considered infidels *(küffar)* and people of ignorance *(cehele-i nası)* who belonged to a heretical sect that deviated from the obligatory precepts of Islam. The *kızılbaş* in particular were singled out as heretics *(rafiza)* and bandits *(eşkıya)* who were repudiators of Allah *(mülhid)*.[10] In Ottoman *fetvas* the *rafiza* were accused of believing that 'Ali was a god and the true successor to the Prophet, and that the first three caliphs were not true imams. Denial of the first three caliphs was a common accusation against the *kızılbaş* in Ottoman documents (Refik 1932; Eberhard 1970, 104–10).[11] Sunni Islam considered *kizılbaş*-ism a heresy against its basic principles, and the penalty for such heresy was death.[12]

The earliest known Ottoman anti-Shi'i *fetvas* were those by Müfti Hamza (Molla Nur al-Din b. Yusuf al-Karasiwi, known as Saru Görez, d. 1521), who held the rank of judge *(kadı)* in Istanbul. His most famous *fetva* was issued in response to a *kızılbaş* revolt in 1511 and 1512. This insurgency was under the command of Shah Kulu, an agent of Shah Isma'il. It began in southwestern Anatolia, where the *kızılbaş* burned and destroyed everything in their path, and extended into the central heartland of the empire. The reverberations of the revolt reached all the way to Istanbul. The rebellion was eventually suppressed, but only after a long struggle that led to the execution and banishment of some

10. Irène Mélikoff has shown how the use of these terms denoted a particular group of Turkmen who were Twelver Shi'ites who professed extremist views such as the manifestation of Allah to man in human form (*tecelli*) and metempsychosis, or the soul passing into the body of another at death (*tenasüh*) (see Mélikoff 1975, 50. See also Watt 1963, 116, 120).

11. See also Bosworth 1993, 99.

12. In addition to *fetvas,* other Ottoman documents were also filled with vivid descriptions of *kızılbaş* crimes against Islam, such as desecration of Qur'ans, mosques, and other pious institutions, and particularly sexual impropriety.

40,000 *kızılbaş* in Anatolia. Müfti Hamza's *fetva* legitimized the suppression of the *kızılbaş* and sanctioned war with the Safavids, which led to their defeat at Çaldıran. He maintained that the *kızılbaş* were infidels and heretics, and that murdering them was every Muslim's duty. Most important for this study, he adjudged that marriages amongst them, as well as their marriages with others, were not legally valid.[13] Muslims could not inherit from them, and the state could legally confiscate "infidel" property, wives, and children.[14]

Müfti Hamza's declaration that capital punishment was required for unbelief *(küfr)* followed the consensus among classical Islamic legal scholars who, on the basis of several Qur'anic injunctions and many traditions *(ahadith)* of the Prophet, held that the death penalty was required

13. Marriage prohibitions were pronounced from the earliest periods of Islamic history. The caliph 'Umar, who was in power during the conquest of Sassanian-controlled Iraq, forbade marriages between Arabs and Persians (see Nasr 2007, 64). Motzki discusses the predominance of non-Arab *mawalis* as legal scholars in the formative years of Islam and states that Ibrahim b. Yazid b. al-Aswad al-Nakha'i, a second-generation jurist in Kufa, was considered by some biographers to have had a non-Arab father and an Arab mother. He goes on to note that because marriages between non-Arab males and Arab women were disapproved of, they were quite rare in the first century of Islam (see Motzki 1999, ft. 37, 304). A prohibition of marriages between Shi'a and Sunnis also existed between the Banu Huseyn and the Twelver Shi'ite community (*al-Nakhawila*) in Medina. The Banu Huseyn first appears in Medina in the tenth century around the time of the Fatimid conquest of Egypt in 969 CE (see Ende 1997, 293).

14. *"dahi nikahları gerekse kendülerden ve gerekse gayrden alsunlar batıldur"*; *"dahi bunlar kimseden miras yemek yoktur"*; and *"bunların (ricallerin katl idüb) mallarını ve nisalarını ve evladlarını guzat-ı İslam arasında kismet ide,"* reproduced in Tekindağ 1967, 55 (see also Mélikoff 1975, 51). Scholars have long held that the Ottomans increasingly intervened in domestic affairs in the nineteenth century, partially as a result of the Tanzimat Reforms, to a degree that had not occurred in early periods. While this fact is not disputed, these sixteenth *fetvas* do suggest that such interventions also took place as early as the sixteenth century, albeit with a different degree of legislation and enforcement. Certainly we cannot analyze the demographic importance of marriage in the premodern period of Ottoman history within the same framework that we can discuss it in the nineteenth century. Further research is necessary, however, to see if a comparative study would be feasible.

for unbelievers.[15] Calling for the death penalty, however, even for those who had repented, was a very severe sanction, because classical scholars—particularly Malik—allowed an apostate *(mürted)* to be given time to rethink his apostasy and to repent and return to Islam (Halkin 1935, 224; Khadduri 1955, 149–52).

In pronouncing marriage forbidden amongst the *kızılbaş* and between them and others, Müfti Hamza was following the long tradition of Ash'ari scholarship, one of whose most brilliant exponents, 'Abd al-Kathir ibn-Tahir al-Baghdadi, held that an unorthodox Muslim man could not marry an orthodox woman. Likewise, an orthodox man could not marry a woman from a heretical sect (Seelye 1919, 12–13, 30). Al-Baghdadi also held that a Muslim could not inherit from an apostate, and his property could be confiscated as spoils of war. Opinions of the classical scholars diverged, however, on the seizure and enslavement of wives and children. In this matter, the Ottomans followed the rulings of Abu-Hanifa, who permitted enslavement on the basis of a precedent set by Khalid ibn al-Walid, who enslaved the wives and children of the followers of Musaylima after he had been defeated and killed (Halkin 1935, 224, and note 4, 225).

Müfti Hamza's *fetva* reflected the tone of anti-Shi'i *fetvas* that were to follow in the sixteenth century. Kemalpaşazade (Ibn-i Kemal), who was Şeyhülislam from 1526 to 1533 during the reign of Süleyman II, confirmed that killing Shi'a was legal, and wars against them were also permitted because they could be equated with wars against other "enemy religions" (Altunsu 1972, 17–20; Saray 1990, 20). Their marriages were invalid, and confiscating their property was legal. Perhaps the most famous anti-Shi'i *fetvas* were those of Ebussuud, the Şeyhülislam who served from 1545 to 1574.[16] Because of his long service as chief müfti, as well as his close

15. According to al-Baghdadi, three crimes required the death sentence—adultery in marriage, reprisal for a murdered person who was one's equal, and apostasy (see Halkin 1935, 216).

16. By the late sixteenth century, the şeyhülislam had attained the position as head of all the ulema. He was in a position equal to the grand vizier *(sadrazam),* and had become a member of the Imperial Council *(Divan-ı Hümayun).* In addition, the şeyhülislam also acted as an advisor to the sultan and to the grand vizier. He judged

personal relationship with the sultans Süleyman I (1520–1566) and Selim II (1566–1574), the Office of the Şeyhülislam was institutionalized and integrated into the state machinery, which allowed Ebussuud a measure of power over the affairs of the state. The anti-Safavid rhetoric of his *fetvas* also carried an authority not seen before or since. These *fetvas* closely paralleled contemporary imperial orders relating to the suppression of the *kızılbaş*, and, as a result, a direct connection can be noted between the policies of the state and his legal rulings (Imber 1979, 245–73).

Ebussuud's charges of apostasy against the *kızılbaş* were issued to support government domestic policies and various campaigns fought against the Safavids. In his *fetva* collections the *kızılbaş* were listed under the heading of apostates *(mürtedler).* He charged them with unbelief, and repeatedly called them heretics who deviated from the right path *(ilhad)* because they cursed the companions of the Prophet. Ebussuud's *fetva* in 1548 compared the *kızılbaş* with both the apostates who turned against Muhammad and his companions in the early years after having converted to Islam, and with the *khawarij,* a group who supported 'Ali and then turned against him in his quest for rightful leadership of the community (Düzdağ 1983, 109–11).[17] The comparison with these groups was intended to compare the Shi'a to persons who had been held up as heretics in classical Sunni heresiography.

Ebussuud was in agreement with Müfti Hamza in pronouncing the death sentence on infidels as punishment for such heresy. He justified the penalty by firmly basing his decision on principles of classical Sunni jurisprudence. He pronounced that even Ahmad ibn-Hanbal allowed "killing this group [which] is more important than killing other groups," because like the false prophet Musaylima they led Muslims to error (Seeley 1919,

---

cases brought before him, and he participated in discussions on matters of state. He was authorized to appoint all high-ranking *ulema.* The sultan went to him for his religious ruling in important matters concerning the state. In theory the şeyhülislam had final authority over the actions of the government. For the seminal study of Ebussuud and the Office of the Şeyhülislam, see Repp 1986.

17. See also Imber 1979, 271; Masters 1991, 4–8; and Tucker 1996, 18.

32; Düzdağ 1983, 109–11). In referring to the war against Musaylima that led to his murder and the death of his followers, Ebussuud was again basing his decision on the authority of orthodox Sunni doctrine that demanded the death penalty for those who cursed the companions of the Prophet. The proclamation of the penalty of death in the sixteenth-century *fetvas* also undoubtedly evinced the particular insecurities of the Ottomans, who were faced with a serious geopolitical challenge from the Safavids. Their solution was to maintain their own religious and political domination and to sanction death for all who followed and supported Shi'ism.

Ebussuud's most important pronouncement (for the purpose of this study) was his declaration that marriage in accordance with the Shari'a was not permitted with a heretic and would incur severe punishment *(ta'zir-i şedid)* (Düzdağ 1983, 118). Müfti Hamza's prohibition of marriages between Sunnis and Shi'ites was thus confirmed and strengthened by Ebussuud.

After Ebussuud, anti-*kızılbaş fetvas* continued to be issued in support of persecutions of the *kızılbaş* and wars with the Safavids . In many of these cases, the prohibition of marriage was reaffirmed. In 1578, as the Ottoman army was preparing for war with the Safavids, they ordered a purge of the *kızılbaş.* At this time the governor of Baghdad sent a report stating that there were many heretics and "unbelievers" (Safavid sympathizers) in the province. This area had a large Shi'ite population, and the Ottomans questioned their loyalty. At the same time, a domestic revolt occurred that shook the foundations of the government. A man appeared among the Turkmen tribes in southeastern Anatolia who claimed to be Shah Isma'il, and he gathered many followers who terrorized the countryside. The leader of this "false Isma'il" revolt, as the insurrection was to become known, was suspected of being an agent of the Safavids, sent to divert the Ottoman army from its campaign against the Shi'i state. It was in this period of unrest and war that Sheikh Seyyid Mutahhar declared, "as for this group who are called *kızılbaş,* may Allah eradicate them and ruin them."[18] In the tradition of earlier *fetvas,* he allowed the imposition of the death penalty

18. Tucker 1996, 18, citing Eberhard 1970, 219–30, a German translation of *Mushtamil al-Akawil.*

for their crime of cursing the companions of the Prophet. He also warned against marriages between the *kızılbaş* and Sunni Muslims.[19]

A few years later, in 1581, a government order was sent to officials to help them search out, identify, and detain those who might be *kızılbaş* or Safavi sympathizers. This order described five characteristics that could be used to identify a *kızılbaş:*

> First: they curse and revile the Four Chosen Friends.
>
> Second: they openly address Muslims with the words, *"Yezid geldi."*
>
> Third: they assemble at night, bringing wives and daughters to their assemblies, where they have disposal of each other's wives and daughters.
>
> Fourth: they know neither prayer nor fasting.
>
> Fifth: they never call their sons Abu Bakr, 'Umar or 'Uthman. (Gölpinarlı 1955; Imber 1979, 261)

This order clearly delineated "orthodox" opinion that the *kızılbaş* were transgressors against the true principles of Sunni Islam; for example, their refusal to pray or fast, and their cursing of the "Four Chosen Companions" (the three immediate successors to Muhammad and the Ottoman sultan). The *kızılbaş'* usage of the words *"Yezid geldi"* referred to the Shi'i hatred of Yezid, the son of Mu'awiya, and the second Umayyad caliph, who planned the murder of 'Ali's two sons. The government order stressed Shi'i animosity toward Sunni authority by highlighting their comparison of the sultan with Yezid.

In addition to their transgressions of Islamic principles, Ottoman authorities often accused the *kızılbaş* of immoral behavior. Separation of the sexes was not strictly observed among Sufi sects in Anatolia, and it was not unusual for them to include wives and daughters in ceremonies. Such activity could easily, where necessary, lead to accusations of sexual impropriety.[20] Ottoman religious authority's view of sexual impropriety may

19. Imber 1979, 253–54, citing the *Mühimme Defterleri;* Finkel 2005, 181.

20. In fact, some scholars contend that the Ottomans knew very little about the Shi'a other than information they had gathered about the tribes in border areas. Their

have been influenced by classical orthodox scholarship that accused specific sects such as the Maimuniyah and the Khawarij of unlawful sexual relations with women in the forbidden degrees of consanguinity (Seeley 1919, 29; Halkin 1935, 105–6). But Ottoman legal scholars also may have had access to fourth- and fifth-century AH (tenth and eleventh century CE) Hanafi heresiographic literature from eastern Iran and Transoxiana. In this literature, Sunni scholars denounced the Shi'a and other sects as heretical because of their practice of temporary *(mut'a)* marriages. Such sexual impropriety allegedly included making women available to men without formal marriages; contracting marriages without guardians or witnesses; and permitting marriages to one's granddaughters and nieces (Lewinstein 1994, 584, 597–98).[21]

In the imperial orders to officials, Ottoman authorities were trying to draw a picture of the *kızılbaş* and the Shi'a, not only as unbelievers, but as people who were a threat to the empire and to the greater Muslim community because of their anti-Sunni activities and their immoral behavior. By placing the *kızılbaş* and the Shi'a in such a position in the community, the authorities could more easily justify their repressive activities and could call on all "true believers" to participate in the suppression of these "infidels." In denying the right of Sunnis and Shi'ites to marry, the Ottoman government and religious authorities were creating a separation between Muslims that had little basis in Islamic law. This exclusion, although originally based on accusations of heresy, was in fact fueled by both domestic and geopolitical concerns. Once the prohibition

research shows that the Ottoman accusations of unbelief against the Shi'a were in fact based on the activities of the dervishes in Anatolia, whose practices had many elements of pre-Islamic shamanist beliefs (see Walsh 1962, 206; see also Mélikoff 1982, 142–54).

21. Ottoman scholars, from as early as the fifteenth century, may have had access to such material. From the reign of Mehmed the Conqueror through the period of Süleyman I, sultans carried on a policy of importing scholars from other regions into the center for religious learning. Nevertheless, more research needs to be undertaken to establish a direct connection.

was established in the *fetva* literature, it was routinely called upon as warranted by geopolitical circumstances.

In designating the *kızılbaş* and Safavids as heretics, the Ottoman government was responding to very real political challenges to state centralization and expansion. The hegemonic rise of the Ottoman Empire had encountered no serious challenges for over two centuries, until the establishment of the Shiʿi-Safavid state. Not only did the Safavids contest territory in Anatolia and Iraq, but they also presented the first great geopolitical challenge and forced the Ottomans to defend their position as the legitimate rulers over the entire Muslim community. As a result of this challenge, the Ottomans had to define their own theory of empire based on the exclusion of their Shiʿi neighbors on their eastern border.

The threat to the empire from Safavid loyalists in Anatolia and the border regions did not cease after the sixteenth century. In the seventeenth century, there were periodic uprisings and infiltrations by agents of the shahs in Ottoman territory. Yet, to date, no documents have been discovered that show interest by Ottoman officials and the religious establishment in reasserting the prohibition of marriages. If indeed none exist, then the question remains why the prohibition was not reasserted or strengthened by central religious authorities. Zarinebaf-Shahr has suggested that the definitions of heresy put forth in the sixteenth century were well understood and institutionalized by that time, and there was therefore no need to produce an official treatise on heresy that would have included a prohibition of marriage (1997, 12). If there were no reassertions of the prohibition, perhaps the original reason for the rhetorical package designating the Shiʿa as heretics was eventually abandoned as the desire for a unified community disintegrated over time. It may therefore come as a surprise to discover that the prohibition continued on the local level during this period.

In the eighteenth century, the prohibition of marriages between Sunnis and Shiʿites was again asserted by a *fetva* from the Chief Mufti of Damascus. Although this was not a pronouncement emanating from the central Office of the Şeyhülislam, it was important, nonetheless, because of the time and place it was issued and the motivation behind its declaration. Local officials had become concerned over the apparent spread of intermarriage between Ottoman Sunnis and Persian Shi'i pilgrims, who were journeying to Mecca and Medina and often settling for a period of time in Damascus. The question of Persians' access to the holy cities of Mecca and Medina had always been an issue between the two governments. During periods of war, the cities of Arabia, as well as the sacred Shi'i shrines in southern Iraq, were closed to Persian pilgrims. In peacetime the Ottoman government strictly controlled Persian access by carefully delineating overland routes that would steer their caravans away from Baghdad and the shrine cities. The Ottomans were aware that the Safavids sent spies and agitators in the caravans who were to contact loyalists in Ottoman territory to create disturbances. Ottoman control of Persian travelers was clearly presented in a rescript circa 1564–1565 during the reign of Sultan Süleyman I:

> It is not permissible to enter my well-guarded territories at any time outside of the [pilgrimage] season. . . . May they all appear at the previously determined time. Their arrival should be reported to [the Ottoman authorities] so that [the pilgrims] can be met at the border. (Faroqhi 1994, 128)

The right of Persian pilgrims to make the pilgrimage had been established by the Treaty of Kurdan of 1746, which ended five years of warfare between the Ottomans and Afghans who had taken control of Safavid Iran. The treaty established a working relationship, allowing the exchange of ambassadors between the two states. Persians were permitted to appoint an *emir'l-hac* for pilgrims on their yearly journey to the holy cities via routes through Baghdad and Damascus. They were also allowed to visit the shrines sacred to Shi'i Islam in Iraq. Damascus remained one of the main routes for pilgrims coming from the east. If pilgrims arrived too late to join the caravans, they would settle in Damascus until the following year (or sometimes permanently) rather than risk traveling over insecure roads where pilgrims were often attacked by bandits. Whether settling temporarily or permanently, Persian Shi'ites apparently intermarried with Ottoman Sunni women, which was the cause for concern among Ottoman officials.

War again broke out between the Ottomans and Persians in 1774 and lasted until 1779. The Ottomans were in a weakened position after wars with Russia when Karim Khan, the head of the Shi'i Zand tribe, took control of Iran and established the Zand dynasty (1751–1794). Karim Khan immediately began sending raiding parties into eastern Anatolia and captured Basra in April of 1776. Sultan Abdülhamid I (1774–1789) sent his army against the Zand, repelling them from Basra one year later, and against Ömer Paşa al-Da'ud, the governor of Baghdad (1764–1775), who refused to offer assistance to the Ottomans. The war was justified by a juridical opinion that declared the Zand as heretics and their attack on Basra as arrogance (Shaw 1976, 1:254; Finkel 2005, 407). Against this backdrop, local religious officials revisited the prohibition of marriages between Ottoman women and Iranian men.

The *ulama* of Damascus in the eighteenth century often played an essential role in political events, and defended Damascenes against arbitrary behavior and injustice. 'Ali bin Muhammad al-Muradi (d. 1771), a Hanafi *mufti,* for example, was greatly loved by the populace for defending them against oppression by officials. He was a member of one of two local families (the other being the 'Imadi family) who were *mufti*s in Damascus for most of the latter half of the eighteenth and the beginning of the nineteenth centuries. Al-Muradi was the *mufti* between 1758 and 1771, succeeding Hamid Efendi al-'Imadi (1725–1758). During his period in office, al-Muradi abolished arbitrary regulations and excessive taxation on Damascene merchants (Shamir 1963, 9; Rafeq 1966, 49; Tucker 2000, 21; Weismann 2007, 75). At the request of a Damascus judge, al-Muradi issued a treatise that invalidated all marriages between Shi'a and Sunnis.[22]

22. The treatise was titled *al-Rawd al-ra'id fi 'adam sihhat nikah ahl al-Sunna lil rawafid.* It is undated but apparently written between 1758 and 1771, the years when al-Muradi was mufti in Damascus (see Pococke 1745, II.i 136; Rafeq 1966, 60; Salati 1993, 141; and my personal correspondence with Professor Abdul-Karim Rafeq, 15 July 2009).

Although additional information about the marriage prohibition in the eighteenth century remains scarce,[23] we have one additional source from this century that suggests a history of reciprocity within one Shiʿite community. The al-Nakhawila community in Medina first appears in Ottoman sources in the seventeenth century. They, however, claimed that their descendents were present in Medina from the earliest years of Islam, when they worked in the date palm groves of al-Hasan ibn ʿAli, the grandson of Muhammad and the second Shiʿi imam. A Medina notable of the eighteenth century, ʿAbd al-Rahman al-Ansari (d. circa 1783) noted that in the earliest years of Islam they did not allow their women to marry Sunni men, and their men also could not marry Sunni women. An Ottoman Turkish official stationed in Medina, Eyyub Sabri, also wrote circa 1888 or 1889 that in early Islam the local Sunni population did not marry the daughters of the al-Nakhawila, nor did they marry their own daughters to men from the Twelver Shiʿite tribe (Ende 1997, 302–5).

Although the Damascus case is only one example of a local pronouncement of the marriage prohibition, it is nevertheless instructive in two respects. The prohibition did not emanate as state policy from the central religious establishment, but was issued by local religious officials in response to larger geopolitical concerns. This treatise continued the rhetorical discourse of heresy from the sixteenth century in designating the Shiʿa as heretics *(rawafid)* and reaffirmed the prohibition of marriage between Sunnis and Shiʿa. It is interesting to note also that this prohibition was restated not long after the Ottomans and Persians had appeared on the road to accommodation with the Treaty of Kurdan in 1746. It might have been expected that, within the process of normalizing relations, personal status issues between Ottomans and Persians would be

23. Scant scholarship has been produced on *fetva* collections in eighteenth-century Syria. There are four volumes of *fatawa* by Muhammad Khalil al-Muradi, ʿAli bin Muhammad al-Muradi's son, in the Zahiriyya/Asad Library, that have yet to be studied and analyzed. This is just one collection from one jurist. Many more collections abound because Syrian jurists came into growing disagreement with Ottoman law during this century. (I thank Professor Abdul-Karim Rafeq for the above information relayed in personal correspondence, 23 July 2009.)

normalized as well. A new set of geopolitical concerns arose, however, with the appearance of the Zand in the late eighteenth century. The fuel for the reassertation of the marriage prohibition revolved around questions of contested territory and influence in the border regions of both empires, which led to a sense of immediate internal threats to territorial integrity and loyalty of the population in the eastern Ottoman provinces. The Ottomans would continue to reconsider and strengthen the prohibition when geopolitical circumstances demanded such action. In the nineteenth century, geopolitical concerns became even more acute, and the central government recovered its voice in proclaiming the prohibition of marriages. It is these concerns that will now be addressed.

Buyruldu-ı ʿAli of 1822 and Rising Tensions on the Ottoman-Iranian Frontier

On 11 Rebiyülahir 1237 AH (5 January 1822), Sultan Mahmud II (1808–1839) proclaimed a Supreme Mandate (*Buyruldu-ı ʿAli),* "Concerning the Prohibition of Marriage with Iranians."[24] The mandate was proclaimed at a time of both rapidly changing circumstances in the empire as Mahmud II sought to consolidate and centralize his regime, as well as rising external tensions with Iran, which tried to achieve territorial advances against the Ottomans to compensate for their losses to Russia.

The framers of the mandate of 1822 asserted that the prohibition of marriage had been in force since "ancient times." Such a declaration, harking back to traditional anti-Shiʿi rhetoric, was used to lend legitimacy and authority to the prohibition by invoking continuity with the past. The mandate also employed the traditional language of sectarian division by declaring that the sultan was the upholder of the "true" Islam as well as the moral leader of the larger Muslim community. In emphasizing the sultan's essential role as leader of the faithful, the Ottomans, in fact, were reinforcing their awareness of the geopolitical reality—that unity of the Muslim community was not a political reality. The Ottoman worldview, with respect

24. Başbakanlık Osmanlı Arşivi, hereafter BOA, *Ecnebi Defterleri* 43/1, 36–37. See also appendix A.

to their leadership of the *umma* and the Shi'a's place within that community, understood that the Iranians were an irrevocably separate empire and relations should proceed within that context. Specific issues of *realpolitik* between the two empires not only allowed this prohibition to continue, but also demanded its reassertion and strengthening by imperial edict.

In contrast to Ottoman recognition of the Iranian empire's legitimacy, as stated in the 1746 Treaty of Kurdan, the 1822 mandate continued to use the rhetoric of the earlier *fetva* literature. The mandate specifically designated as heretics *(rafiza)* the Shi'a, Iranians, people of ignorance *(cehele-ı nası),* and people of unknown lineage *(meçhulünnesep eşhas),* all of whom had strayed from the true path of Islam and were prohibited from marrying Ottomans. The mandate, additionally, was much more specific than the *fetvas* about who was prohibited from marrying, the reasons for enacting the prohibition, and the mechanisms for its enforcement. Marriages with the aforesaid groups were expressly considered as "deviating from the obligatory precepts *(usul-i mefruzat)* of Islam," and all Muslims were "required to know the principles concerning the Islamic religion." The specificity of the title of the mandate, however, clearly signifies that its primary intent was to prohibit marriages with Iranians, and the religious establishment was given the primary responsibility for enforcing the prohibition. The mandate charged religious officials, particularly *kadıs* and imams, with the duty of prohibiting marriages between Ottomans and Iranians by investigating all marriages at the time they were contracted. Local authorities were instructed to be particularly diligent in assuring that Ottoman-Sunni women did not marry Iranians. Religious authorities who did not investigate, or who were negligent in their duties and permitted such contracts of marriage, and fathers or guardians who permitted their daughters to marry persons who were *rafiza,* Iranians, Shi'a, or of unknown lineage would be "strongly punished." The investigation by religious officials was to ensure that there would be no doubt about the family origins of those getting married.[25]

Many geopolitical issues between the Ottoman and Iranian empires during the nineteenth century were continuations of long-standing dis-

25. Ibid.

agreements between these states. Ottoman and Iranian animosity had resulted in numerous battles and border disputes, and shifting control of territory in Iraq during the previous centuries. Although many treaties had attempted to normalize relations between these two empires, unresolved issues remained. The 1822 mandate was declared in the midst of a geopolitical crisis—another major Ottoman-Iranian border conflict.

Border conflicts had not ended with the Amasya Treaty of 1555. That treaty was broken in 1623 when the Safavids reoccupied Iraq. Sultan Murad IV (1623–1640) led a massive war effort and successful repelled the Safavids, recapturing Baghdad in 1638. The Treaty of Zuhab (1639) ended the war and held the peace until the fall of the Safavids in 1722. It regulated the borders of the empires and affirmed Ottoman control over Baghdad, Basra, and Mosul. The Ottomans and Safavids would continue to contest other strategic parts of the border, but the frontiers delineated in Zuhab would remain virtually unchanged for the next two hundred years. In future negotiations, the 1639 treaty remained the point of reference.[26]

A century of peace between the Ottomans and Iranians resulted from stability in Iran in the late Safavid period. With the abdication of Shah Sultan Husayn on 22 October 1722, however, the Safavid dynasty came to an end. The invasion of Iran by Afghans resulted in a long seven months of siege and an inability to unify the country. The Afghans were soon overthrown by Nadir Khan of the Turkmen Afshar tribe, and the former stable truce was lost between the Ottoman and Iranian empires. Nadir Khan immediately turned against the Ottomans and besieged Baghdad in 1733, forcing the Ottomans to sue for peace. They both agreed to return to the borders of 1639. In 1743, however, Nadir Shah (by this time he had declared himself the First Shah of the Afshar Dynasty) turned again to Iraq, where he attacked the Ottoman fortress in Mosul. Peace was again achieved by the Treaty of Kurdan in 1746, which established

26. Contested parts of the border included the shoals and islands in and around the Shatt al-Arab, as well as the Panjawin and Zuhab highlands on the eastern border of Iraq and Khuzistan in the south (Hurewitz 1975, 25–28; Finkel 2005, 222).

a new basis for political recognition between the Ottoman and Iranian empires. In this treaty, the Ottoman Empire recognized the legitimacy of the Iranian state and abandoned its long-standing depiction of the Shi'a as heretics whose destruction by the Ottomans was justified by Qur'anic injunction. As mentioned earlier, Iranian pilgrims were allowed safe access through Baghdad and Damascus to perform the pilgrimage to the holy cities of Arabia. Most important, for the first time, the Iranian empire was allowed status equal to that accorded other Muslim states (Aitchison 1909, appendixes, iii–xi; Finkel 2005, 363–64).

Iranian border skirmishes and raids into Iraq continued, however. Between 1821 and 1822, the Iranians successfully captured Erzurum and Beyazit in the Ottoman east, and moved toward Bitlis and Diyarbakir in the heart of southern Anatolia. The Iranians were stopped only when an outbreak of cholera forced them to seek peace. The Treaties of Erzurum of 1823 and 1848 ended this conflict by reaffirming the provisions of the 1746 Treaty of Kurdan and providing no change in boundaries (Danismend 1972, 59; Shaw and Shaw 1977, 16–17; Masters 1991, 3–16).[27] In the first Treaty of Erzurum, signed in July of 1823, both states averred that they would not interfere in the internal affairs of the other, and Iran agreed not to meddle in Baghdad and Kurdistan. Iranian pilgrims were allowed free access without extra taxation to the holy cities in Arabia, as well as to the shrine cities of southern Iraq (Tucker 1996, 35). The sultan and the shah recognized each other as equal, legitimate heads of sovereign states. The treaties did not mention the sultan's role as "leader of all Muslims"; instead, both the sultan and the shah were afforded the use of the title of "caliph." Iranians living in the Ottoman Empire were, for the first time, recognized as subjects of a foreign state—a recognition long accorded subjects of European states. Iran was, therefore, the first, and only, Muslim state to be allowed to join the ranks of European capitulatory states. As a result, Iran was included in the "Registers of Foreigners"

27. See Hurewitz 1975, 219–21 for a translation of the "Treaty of Peace (Erzurum): The Ottoman Empire and Persia," 28 July 1823. See also Aitchison 1909, lx–lxi.

(Ecnebi Defterleri), which had previously dealt only with matters concerning European capitulatory nations that came to the attention of the Ottoman government (Masters 1991, 11). Issues concerning Iranians were now included in this collection, and it is within the Register of Foreigners that we find the 1822 mandate "Concerning the Prohibition of Marriage with Iranians."

Iranians were given limited capitulatory rights within the empire, including the right for the Iranian government to intervene in the domestic affairs of the Ottoman Empire when a matter concerned its citizens. Complete extraterritorial rights given Europeans were not accorded the Iranians with regard to judicial independence, however. Iranians involved in commercial or criminal actions with Ottomans were still tried in Ottoman courts according to Ottoman law, but they were allowed to have their own representatives in the court. Iranian pilgrims were allowed to settle disputes among themselves, and, where necessary, certain cases could be referred directly to the Sublime Porte for adjudication. The shah was permitted to appoint consuls in the empire "wherever the interest of commerce or the protection of merchants or subjects of Persia render it necessary—with the exception of the holy cities of Mecca and Medina, and the Porte will confer on the said Consuls the privileges due to their official character, and which are enjoyed by Consuls of other friendly states" (Aitchison 1909, lv, lxi; Masters 1991, 9–11, 14; Tucker 1996, 34–36).

The primary goal of these treaties was to establish the final borders between the two empires. The first Treaty of Erzurum of 1823, however, left many border issues unresolved, including sovereignty over Khuzistan and the boundary between Ottoman Basra and the Persian province of Shushter. Continuing minor interventions, counterinterventions, and protests on each side occurred after the 1823 treaty. Between 1843 and 1847, a Persian-Ottoman mixed boundary commission was established, with the mandate to produce a border agreement. After four years of negotiations, under pressure from Britain and Tsarist Russia, who had vested interests in the region, the second Treaty of Erzurum was signed on 31 May 1847 and went into effect the following year. This treaty was intended to settle the final boundaries and all differences over frontiers, tribal matters, and navigation in the Shatt al-Arab. There was still no precisely defined border, so Article 3 established a Joint Delimitation Commission in order to begin negotiation and adjust conflicting claims about the final borders. Because little progress was being made in the border dispute, Britain and Tsarist Russia joined in mediating between the two empires. Britain, in particular, had critical interests in seeing a settlement of the issue. Lack of delimitation was the final obstacle to British imperial interests in India, which demanded an extension of the Indo-European Telegraph Line (IETL) from London to Karachi. The Europe-Baghdad and Tehran-India portions of the line were complete. Between 1863 and 1865, the British government carried on extensive negotiations with the Qajar Shah, Nasir al-Din (1848–1896), and the Ottoman Sultan, Abdülaziz (1861–1876) in order to find a solution to the border dispute so the final section of the transcontinental line could be completed. At issue was seventeen miles of land between the Ottoman-Iraqi outpost of Khanaqin and the Iranian outpost of Qasr-i Shirin. The Ottomans and Qajars both claimed sovereignty over these seventeen miles of territory and over the inhabitants, who were mostly nomadic tribes that paid taxes and provided soldiers. After two years of negotiation, the two sides found a mechanism by which the telegraph line could be completed without solving the ultimate problem of fixing the borders. The agreement allowed for alternating iron (Ottoman) and wooden (Iranian) poles to be built by the British at Ottoman and Iranian expense. In addition, a neutral line was fixed and guarded by both Ottoman and Iranian patrols (al-Izzi 1972, 1–22).[28]

28. See also Shahvar 2007, 28, 33–34, 40–41. Britain had intervened in Ottoman-Iranian affairs as early as 1823 when it attempted to help end this war, and again in 1843 in order to prevent another war between the two empires. In consideration of its commercial interests in India, Britain sought to use Iraq and Iran as a buffer against Russian ambitions to push southward in search of warm-water ports. The British government realized that war between the Ottoman and Qajar empires meant a weakening of these two states and an opportunity for Russia to take territorial advantage of this rivalry.

Ottoman and Iranian commissioners continued work to determine the exact point where the frontier should be fixed. After more than twenty years, no permanent settlement was achieved, and the commission was finally suspended. The boundary between the two empires continued to be disputed throughout the nineteenth and into the twentieth century. This was a legacy from the previous centuries and the many treaties negotiated by the two states that had failed to find a workable formula for a mutual recognition of borders (Kuneralp 1987, 71–76). On 21 December 1911, the "Tehran Protocol" established a new joint commission to again try to find a solution to the border disagreements. The Commission finished its work on 26 October 1914, detailing the frontiers and finally settling the border as fixed and not liable to further contest or revision. Both the Ottomans and the Iranians formally accepted the demarcation of their borders (al-Izzi 1972, 14–17).

2

The Challenge of Shi'i Conversion Activity to Ottoman Control of Iraq

THE PROHIBITION OF MARRIAGES between Ottoman women and Iranian men was enacted against the backdrop of one of the most important geopolitical issues between the Ottoman and Iranian Empires—the conversion of the Sunni population of Iraq to Shi'ism. The importance of conversion to the Ottoman government was evident in Mahmud II's imperial mandate of 1822: "Concerning the Prohibition of Marriage to Iranians." The mandate emphatically stated that "ignorant" Muslims might change schools [from Sunni to Shi'i Islam] as the result of these marriages. Conversion to Shi'ism would "God forbid, cause suffering in this world and the next" *(cehele-i ehl-i islamın tagayyür-i mezhebiyle maazallahüteala iki alemde müptela-i hüsran olmasını),* a serious charge that emphasized penalties in the here and now and damnation in the afterlife.[1] Such a forceful declaration continued the Ottoman tradition of using accusations of heresy in the service of geopolitical realities. Although Mahmud II recognized the different "nationality" of Iranians both in the mandate and on the level of *realpolitik,* when geopolitical circumstances warranted, the sultan's worldview saw Sunni Islam as the "true" religion and Shi'ism as a heresy.

The issue of conversion in the context of the prohibition of marriages was directly connected with two major interrelated geopolitical concerns in the 1820s: the major war between Iranians and Ottomans that ended with the Treaty of Erzurum of 1823 (discussed in the previous chapter),

1. BOA, *Ecnebi Defterleri*, 43/1, 36–37. See also appendix A.

and Ottoman control over its eastern border provinces where Shiʿi *ulema* were increasing their attempts to convert the population.[2] As discussed before, the Ottomans and the Iranians had long contested the frontier territory of Iraq. Although the Ottomans maintained that the Iraqi provinces were Ottoman territory, the Safavid (1501–1722) and Qajar (1794–1925) shahs periodically laid claim to the right to protect both the Shiʿi population of Iraq and the shrine cities of Najaf, Karbala', Kadhimiyya, and Samarra', which were particularly important to Shiʿites both inside and outside the empire. For centuries, control over provinces that were distant from the center of Ottoman administration had been extremely difficult, and for long periods Iraq remained under minimal central control. The Basra province in southern Iraq, in particular, was a difficult district to rule because the people there maintained a local identity that did not translate to allegiance to a central government that was so far away.

Before the late eighteenth century, there is little evidence of any concerted Shiʿi effort to convert the Sunni population in Iraq. Although in earlier centuries there certainly were Shiʿa in these provinces, most of them were Arabs and they were a minority who lived mainly in the urban centers. During the two periods of Safavid occupation, from 1508 to 1533 and from 1622 to 1638, Persian Shiʿi merchants migrated and settled in major towns such as Baghdad, Karbala', and Najaf. But it was not until the eighteenth century—first when the Afghans occupied Isfahan, and later when Nadir Shah embarked on his program of Sunni-Shiʿi reconciliation—that hundreds of Shiʿi *ulema* sought refuge in the shrine cities and in Baghdad and Basra. Between 1727 and 1763 the shrine cities became centers for Shiʿi scholarship that attracted many Persian *ulema* and students. In 1722, the Shiʿi state of Awadh (Oudh) in North India began an annual contribution of ten thousand pounds sterling for charitable causes

2. Concern over conversion in the empire was not limited to the Iraqi provinces. The Reform Rescript of 1856 *(Islahat Fermanı)* had opened the door to Christian missionary activity throughout the empire, and by midcentury the problem of conversion in general was an empire-wide concern. See Deringil 1998, who deals with the issue of conversion throughout his book.

in the shrine cities. This great wealth gave rise to an influx of Shi'i *ulema* and students into the cities. These political and economic factors afforded the Shi'i *ulema* a large measure of independence from Ottoman control over the administrative affairs of these cities (Cole 1986, 461–80).[3]

In the late eighteenth century, Shi'i conversion activity became more noticeable. Partially as the result of neglect and inattention from the Iraqi Mamluk governors, the Shi'i *ulema* in the shrine cities were able to reinforced their independence and began actively seeking converts among the Arab tribal confederations that had migrated to southern Iraq after attacks by followers of Ibn 'Abd ul-Wahhab. These tribes formed the basis of Iraq's Arab Shi'ite population. Ottoman officials noticed the increase in Shi'i conversion activity and considered it a threat to their control of the three provinces in Iraq.[4] They were also aware of their Mamluk governors' lack of attention to conversion activities.

Mamluk rule in the Ottoman Iraqi provinces began with a father-and-son dynasty, Hasan Paşa (1702–1724) and Ahmad Paşa (1724–1747), whose civil service was composed primarily of Circassian and Georgian youths. The Mamluk regime technically began, however, with the reign of Sulayman Abu-Laylah (1750–1762), a former slave of Georgian origin who trained slaves for the highest civil and military posts. His Georgian Guard was the elite fighting force in the Mamluk structure. With few exceptions, most of the Mamluk rulers of Baghdad and Basra were former slaves from Georgia. They were not, however, a cohesive group, and with no clear lines of succession, power transfers resulted in periods of instability.

The Mamluks pledged loyalty to the sultan in Istanbul and fulfilled a function for the Ottoman government by contributing substantial trade revenues and basic security in strategically important provinces that were far from the center of power. The Mamluk's distance from the center of power contributed to their autonomy. Ottoman armies could

3. See also Çetinsaya 2006, 100.

4. The main confederations who migrated between 1791 and 1801 were the Shammar, 'Anaza, and Zafir (see Nakash 1994, 25–28).

not successfully challenge their power because they had to travel long distances across territory that had no substantial road systems and was often plagued by tribal insurgency. Any military campaigns against the Mamluks would have been financially and militarily risky. The Ottomans were able to finally overturn this dynasty and install their own governors only because of weaknesses during the reign of the last Mamluk governor, Da'ud Paşa (1816–1831), which were caused by wars against the Qajars that created instability in the provinces (Nieuwenhuis 1982, ix, 13–15, 75–77, 87–96).

Da'ud Paşa was particularly tolerant of Shi'i rituals and conversion activity. As a result of his laxity, in the early decades of the nineteenth century, the Shi'i *ulema* intensified their program of conversion. When Mahmud II ascended the throne in 1808, the shrine cities of Najaf and Karbala' were under the total control of the Shi'i *ulema.* Although the ruling class were Sunni notables, a large portion of the population in the southern and eastern parts of the province were Persian, and their allegiance was to Shi'ism and to Iran. These people resented Ottoman attempts to control the province and saw themselves as a religious and ethnic opposition to the Ottoman-Sunni sultan, whom they regarded as a heretic and not rightfully entitled to leadership of the community. Leadership, in their opinion, should fall to the Twelfth Imam (Cole and Momen 1986, 112–43).

The Ottomans recognized that the increase in the Shi'i population might lead to eventual loss of the eastern provinces, and in 1826, Mahmud II attempted to reassert authority and bring the population more closely under the control of the central government. The sultan took various measures to impose direct rule by removing and banishing Da'ud Paşa; installing an Ottoman governor, 'Ali Rıza Paşa (1831–1842); and establishing a permanent standing army in the southern regions.[5] Mahmud's attempt to bring the population of Karbala' under Ottoman control, however, resulted in periodic outbreaks of rioting and rebellion among the Shi'i

5. The Ottomans were able to establish direct rule over Mosul in 1835 (see Shields 2000, 24).

population. In 1835, a serious confrontation erupted between 'Ali Rıza Paşa and the people of Karbala', which had by then become a stronghold for opposition to Ottoman rule. The Shi'i religious leaders, believing that weak rule from Baghdad could not challenge their independence, stirred up hatred of the Sunnis among the Shi'i population. It was clear to the Shi'i leadership that if the Ottomans resumed control of the city, it would threaten their management of the profits resulting from shrine endowments and pilgrimage traffic. They also feared that Sunni law would be reestablished over the Shi'i population, and that the Ottoman government would prohibit Shi'i rituals, particularly the *Muharrem* ceremonies that celebrated the martyrdom of Hüseyn, the grandson of Muhammad. The Shi'i leadership and the population, however, either were not aware of, or misjudged, the strength of Mahmud's centralizing policies. As a result, the people of Karbala' were unable to resist the forces that were sent by the central government. After a long siege, the rebellion was suppressed, and by 1843, Karbala' was once again under Ottoman-Sunni leadership. As the Shi'i *ulema* had feared, Sunni judges were installed and instructed to hear all court cases, including those that involved Shi'i parties. Sunni prayer leaders were reinstated, and the name of the sultan was once again mentioned in Friday prayers. The Ottoman government also exacted heavy financial tolls by levying burdensome customs duties on Iranian merchants working in Ottoman territory. After reasserting control, the Ottomans miscalculated in allowing the Shi'a to continue to perform their *Muharrem* ceremonies.

The Ottomans had historically been tolerant of these ceremonies, and their popularity had grown among the population. 'Ali Rıza, the Ottoman governor, was particularly broadminded about the public aspect of these performances, which were held in mosques, schools, and shrines. The celebrations actually became more widespread, and in subsequent decades their public nature aided the Shi'i *ulema* in their efforts to convert the tribal population.[6] In the middle decades of the nineteenth century,

6. Nakash has suggested that the Ottoman tolerance toward these rituals was an attempt to maintain the loyalty of the population in the face of Muhammad 'Ali's

after a long period of reassertion of direct control over the provinces, the Ottomans embarked on a policy of settling the tribal population. The motivation for this was primarily economic, intended to increase agricultural production and tax revenues in order to support the growing involvement of the empire in the world economy. As a consequence of this settlement policy, Shi'i conversion increased noticeably. A change in the tribal structure that resulted once tribes were settled caused a feeling of displacement and alienation. This factor, plus increased taxation, led to growing antigovernment resentment. As a result, conversion to Shi'ism became an antiestablishment movement in the Iraqi provinces, and increased among the tribal population as they resisted the Ottoman's centralization policies (Nakash 1994, 32–47).[7]

Shi'i propaganda

As mentioned before, Ottoman officials were worried that Shi'ism was increasing in the eastern provinces.[8] This perception was not based on hard census data. The first attempt at statistical analysis of population data occurred in 1831, and was undertaken for a number of purposes. The data were to be used to correct taxation irregularities, and also to regularize conscription registration in order to prepare for the creation of a new army which would replace the Janissaries who had been destroyed as a military force in 1826. A more accurate census was also compiled for non-Muslims who were required to pay the head tax *(cizye)* in lieu of military service. Beyond administrative measures, this census also assessed the numbers of Ottoman subjects of various religions and ethnicities, as well as of Muslim tribal populations and of foreigners living in the empire. The

incursions in the Levant (Nakash 1994, 142–43; see also Calmard 1989, 176; Deringil 1990, 52, 59).

7. In comparing the conversion rates between settled tribes and those that remained nomadic, Nakash has shown that those who did not settle remained predominantly Sunni. He has suggested that Ottoman policy, as much as the efforts of the Shi'i *ulema,* was the cause for the increased conversion rates to Shi'ism.

8. See Deringil 1990; Fortna 2002, 62–67.

1831 census was considered an estimate at best because it was difficult to reach all areas of the empire; there were few trained census takers; Muslim males of military age evaded the tally, and females were not counted (Shaw 1978, 325–26; Karpat 2002, 134, 136).

Tanzimat centralizing reforms increased the demand for statistical analysis. In 1835, a census department *(Ceride-i Nüfus Nezareti)* was created, which lasted for about a decade. Census registrations were periodically carried out in 1835, 1838, 1844, and 1857. In 1858, the government became increasingly involved in daily life and established the Department of Land Registry *(Tahrir-i Emlak Nezareti),* which organized commissions of census specialists to register land and its value, identify the status, occupations and income of individuals, and supply a tax population receipt *(vergi nüfus tezkeresi)* that worked as an identity card as well as detailing the tax obligation of each person (Shaw 1975, 426–27; 1978, 327–28).

In 1868 the government created an office of statistics, which was renamed the General Directorate of Statistics in 1874. Since conscription remained the primary reason for census-taking, only male subjects were counted. Tanzimat reformers had hoped to include non-Muslim males in the count as part of a program to remove the head tax and include them in conscription, but resistance from the religious leaders of the non-Muslim communities, from foreign powers, and from non-Muslim males themselves blocked any possibility of achieving this goal. Foreign consuls were required, nevertheless, to provide lists of the names and residences of their subjects in each part of the empire. A tremendous amount of work was accomplished in the year 1874, but the depositions of Abdülaziz and Murad V, and the accession to the sultanate of Abdülhamid II in 1876, led to a cessation of the count (Shaw 1978, 328–30; Karpat 2002, 134, 137–38).

After the cessation of the Ottoman-Russian War that ended with the Treaty of Berlin in 1878, Sultan Abdülhamid II turned to the census as a component of his modernization program. He revived the old system, hired a French expert, and improved training for specialists. His Regulation of Population Registration of 1878 *(Sicill-i Nüfus Nizamnamesi)* established the framework for data collection for conscription and taxation. Data collection was also necessary to safeguard property, and to ensure financial stability, and municipal order and security. In addition to the conscription and taxation registration, the census was part of a centralization program that was meant to guarantee the economic and financial welfare of the empire. The government, therefore, became more closely involved in the daily lives of its subjects, particularly in the arenas of public order, welfare, security, and health and sanitation, all of which required an accurate registration system (Shaw 1978, 330; Karpat 2002, 134, 137–38).

During the 1880s, the Department of the Census *(Nüfus-i Umumi İdaresi)* was charged with the responsible for commercial and demographic statistics, while the compliation of census data was handed over to the Population Registrar *(Sicill-i Nüfus İdare-i Umumiyesi Müdüriyeti)*. Men were registered by place of birth, residence, age, religion, occupation, marital status, and health, and given identity cards for all legal dealings with the government. Women were included for the first time in the registrars (although those over the age of nine were registered by their husbands, so this information could not be verified). When children were born, they were recorded in a notification certificate *(ilmühaber)*, which was then sent to the district census office. Not all women and children were registered in the census, so they remained undercounted. Registration counts in the 1880s were more complete in the central provinces, but the population was only estimated in the mountains and deserts and in the far-flung three provinces of Iraq. This system changed little during the remaining years of the Hamidian period. The Ottomans attempted to compile complete counts throughout the period, but disparities between numbers of Muslim men and women, and estimates in the mountain and desert regions, show the difficulties in acquiring an accurate count (Shaw 1978, 330–36; Duben and Behar 1991, 15–20; Karpat 2002, 139).

Although the population of the Ottoman Arab provinces was periodically registered in the late nineteenth and early twentieth centuries, the Ottoman system was not capable of counting every member of a household. Ottoman registers were estimates, particularly because methods for updating records of births and deaths were never adequate. The female population was not accurately registered because of lack of access to the women's areas of the home, and children were also not counted because they were not considered full members of the household. Nomadic populations were not systematically included in the registers and their numbers were also estimates (McCarthy 1981, 4–7).

Ottoman population records in the Iraqi provinces of Baghdad, Basra, and Mosul were inaccurate because there was no strong central control necessary to carry out detailed registrations. The Ottomans recognized that their reporting was an undercount by at least two-thirds, that counts of females were wholly inadequate, and also that their counts were only estimates of the overall population. As with other Arab provinces, Shi'i Muslims were not included as a separate category in the Ottoman Iraqi registers. Even if they had been included, it would have been difficult to make a distinction between a Shi'ite who was a foreign national and one who was an Ottoman subject. There were no strong administrative and border controls that could adequately count Sunni and Shi'i tribes that moved across borders in seasonal migrations (McCarthy 1981, 35–41).[9] Although hard data proving an increase in the numbers of people professing Shi'ism in Iraq are not available to scholars today, a British census of 1919 showed that the Shi'a comprised 53 percent of the population, the majority of whom were Arab Shi'a, with Persian Shi'a making up about five percent and Indian Shi'a less than one percent. The British data estimated that 80,000 Persians lived in Iraq in 1919, not including those in mixed marriages (Nakash 1994, 13–17).[10]

The 1822 imperial mandate foresaw the beginning of a problem that was to remain a concern for Ottoman officials until the end of the empire.

9. Although many recent demographic studies of the Arab provinces have relied on foreign sources, McCarthy maintains that these sources are inaccurate and reflect estimates at best (see Çetinsaya 2006, 99).

10. Iranian consuls now settled cases between Iranian litigants. Civil, criminal, and succession matters between Ottomans and Iranians were transferred out of the Ottoman Shari'a courts and were heard in mixed tribunals. Matters of personal status, however, were still under the jurisdiction of the Shari'a courts. Iranian subjects were exempt from taxes levied on Ottoman subjects.

Despite the lack of hard data on conversion, from the mid–nineteenth century onward, the government became increasingly preoccupied with Iranian propaganda and the growth of Shi'ism in the Iraqi provinces. Concern over conversion of the tribes was recorded as early as 1862, when Mehmed Namık Paşa, the governor of Baghdad (1861–1868), requested more Sunni religious scholars for the province. Upon appointing Midhat Paşa governor of Baghdad in 1869, the Porte anticipated that this man, who was well known for his provincial reforms, was also capable of controlling the increase of Shi'ism. When he tried to abolish the *Muharrem* ceremonies, however, he did not meet with much success (Çetinsaya 2006, 101).[11]

Propaganda through the use of printed material would not have presented a serious problem before the mid–nineteenth century. The first official propaganda pamphlet was produced only in the 1820s, on behalf of the Ottoman government. Mahmud II was interested in winning wider support for his program of reform, and he engaged Esad Efendi to write a treatise called "The Basis of Victory" *(Üss-ü Zafer).* This pamphlet was written in the high bureaucratic style of the time, and consequently, because of low literacy rates, it was inaccessible to the public at large and unsuccessful as a propaganda vehicle. In the late eighteenth and early nineteenth centuries, a language-reform movement called for simplifying the syntax and written style of Ottoman Turkish. Many dictionaries and works of grammar and syntax were published, and new schools, such as a civil service school and a faculty of letters, were opened to facilitate the training of government employees in the ever-increasing bureaucracy.

Literacy increased further in the mid- to late nineteenth century as the result of the establishment of official and private printing presses, the publication of numerous government and private newspapers and periodicals, and an increase in the number of books being published. Before 1840 only eleven books were published each year in Istanbul; but by 1908, ninety-nine

11. Midhat Paşa was closely connected with the Tanzimat Reforms, serving on many commissions and councils. In 1855, he proposed a provincial reform program to Grand Vizier Reşid Paşa, which he subsequently had the opportunity to test when he was appointed governor of the Danube province (see Finkel 2005, 463–64).

printers were producing 285 books each year. During the Hamidian period, two Istanbul newspapers printed 12,000 and 15,000 copies each, which increased to 40,000 and 60,000 issues each day after the Young Turk revolution. During the last three decades of the nineteenth century, the growth of secular and Christian missionary schools and a state-sponsored educational system also greatly expanded the level of literacy among the general population. At the beginning of the nineteenth century, perhaps two or three percent of the Muslim population was literate. By the end of the century, the literacy rate had increased to 15 percent (Shaw and Shaw 1977, 112, 250; Quataert 2000, 167–68). Because of this increase, producing propaganda pamphlets became centrally important in Ottoman attempts, not only to control Shiʿi conversion activity in the Iraqi provinces, but also to maintain its position as the primary disseminator of the true fundamentals of the Hanafi school—two concerns that were to become increasingly interrelated. The Hamidian regime attempted to inculcate these fundamentals by controlling religious texts, thereby promoting political and religious loyalty in the face of Shiʿi propaganda (Fortna 2002, 66). In 1902, the government authorized the police, interior, and education ministries to investigate Mahmud and Seyyid, two Iranians who were selling "harmful and prohibited" books to religious students in Beyazit, the center of book sales in Istanbul.[12] As late as 1909, Iranian booksellers were petitioning the government for reimbursement for books and pamphlets that Interior Ministry officials had seized years earlier.[13]

In 1865, the government turned its attention to the distribution of books in the Iraqi provinces that were critical of Sunni Islam. The Ottoman Foreign Ministry *(Hariciye Nezareti)* cited three books—*Esrarü'ş-şehade, Fıkhü'r-rıza,* and *Ayne'l-huyut*—on the thoughts and philosophy of Imam Rıza. Their reports did not specify the nature of Imam Rıza's criticisms of the Sunni religion, but officials were concerned that the books

12. BOA, İrade Hususi 210–49, 16 S/1320 (25 May 1902).

13. BOA, Dahiliye Nezareti Muhaberat-ı Umumiye İdaresi (DH. MUİ) 11–1/72, various dates between 16 Ağustos–24 Ağustos 1325 (29 August–6 September 1909).

could incite "the minds and hearts of the people" *(kulub ve ezhan-ı avamı tahrik edebilmesi)* and sow doubt among the population.[14] The matter was handled at the highest level when the Ottoman Foreign Ministry asked the Iranian government to investigate the issue. The assistant foreign minister of Iran, Mirza Said Han, forwarded the results of the investigation to Hüseyn Han, the Iranian ambassador to Istanbul. These books, the report stated, were indeed printed in a lithograph workshop in Iran and imported into the Ottoman Empire. The investigators maintained that the officials of the publishing house did not "pay careful attention, and the aforesaid persons acted contrary to religious ideas." The report maintained that all Iranians were Twelver Shi'ites, and, in their view, Imam Rıza, a preacher in Baghdad, clearly "despised his own sect by falsely making claims" in the name of the Shi'i sect. The Iranian government was very conciliatory, finding the books to be "insulting" and contrary to the "special peaceful aspiration of the Islamic sultans" and injurious to the "harmony of the two communities who are naturally brothers [and] who are one in belief." The report concluded that if Iranian officials became aware of, and did not prevent, the publication of such books or "pretended to be ignorant" of these publications, they would be subject to punishment.[15]

Ottoman officials considered Imam Rıza one of those "ignorant persons who were not aware of the customs of the religion and who caused grief among the people of Islam." It was the "duty of [Sunni] judges to educate and instruct [such persons]." If such persons acted contrary to the customs of the Shari'a, they would be punished in "accordance with religious law." The Ottomans forbade the publication and distribution of these books within the empire.[16]

The case of Imam Rıza was not an isolated event, however. In 1885, reports multiplied on the growth of Shi'ism. The famous Naqshbandi-Khalidi sheikh Ahmed Ziyaüddin, who lived in the *müezzin's* room of

14. BOA, İrade Hariciye 12380, various dates from 20 Şevvel 1281 (18 March 1865) to 8 Safer 1282 (3 July 1896).

15. Ibid.

16. Ibid.

the Fatma Sultan Cami in Istanbul, had discovered a pamphlet called *Hüseyniye Risalesi,* which was allegedly a propaganda vehicle for Shi'ism. He presented the pamphlet to Ottoman officials, who called for an investigation to determine which publishing house had produced the pamphlet. The officials ordered the confiscation of all existing copies and requested recommendations on how to prohibit such publications.[17] Hoca Ishak Efendi, a scholar known for his studies of heresy, was assigned to investigate the matter and compose a refutation. In his report he stated that two Iranians, Hamza and Hüseyn Baba, were proselytizing and leading "men and women in Istanbul and the villages astray." He suggested that Hüseyn be tried in the Shari'a court and that Hamza be located and arrested so that "persons like these who lead people astray do not settle in the Ottoman state and encourage seditious acts." Hoca Ishak Efendi also found that "up until twenty years ago, the population of Iraq were, in the majority, followers of the Sunni sect." Some fifteen to twenty years earlier, however, the Ottoman government had seized assets that had supported the Sunni *ulema* in Baghdad. It was the lack of Sunni *ulema* that had caused the growth of Shi'ism. He also maintained that thousands of Iranian religious students were proselytizing among the villages and tribes (Çetinsaya 2006, 101).

> Fifteen or twenty years ago, the Valis of Baghdad seized, on behalf of the state treasury, the villages, [the proceeds of] which had been given to the *ulama* for living, and as a result, scholars and *ulama* in Baghdad were altogether destroyed. The Iranians, however, in the three towns [the Atabat] and in Najaf and Karbala', have 5,000–6,000 religious students distributed among villages and among tribes, and teach and inculcate harmful books like this one. As a result, the Sunnis in Iraq remained unawakened.[18]

17. BOA, Yıldız Sadaret Hususı Maruzat (Y.A.HUS) 182–67, 28 Şevvel 1302 (10 August 1885). This archive is the correspondence between the Yıldız Palace and the Chancery of the Grand Vizier (see also Çetinsaya 2006, 101).

18. Çetinsaya 2006, 101–2 citing BOA, İrade Dahiliye 75763, 27 Şevvel 1302 (9 August 1885).

Hoca Ishak Efendi touched on one of the major reasons for the perception that Shi'ism was increasing in Iraq: namely, the lack of Ottoman investment in the provinces in comparison to Shi'i financial support. Although management of the shrine cities was under the Ottoman administration, and those who worked at the shrines were appointed by the central government, the Shi'i *ulema* resided there permanently and wielded great influence. They were extremely wealthy from investment by the Iranian government and money from the Oudh bequest (Cole 1986, 461–80; Çetinsaya 2006, 100). This money was invested in infrastructure projects such as the construction of a canal from the Euphrates that would bring water to Najaf. The money also endowed hostels and libraries, and was distributed to Shi'i converts among the tribes and settled populations as an incentive for conversion. In contrast to the wealth flowing into Shi'i institutions, the Sunni foundation *(vaqıf)* lands that supported Sunni schools and religious officials had been taken over by the government as a result of the centralization policies that began with Mahmud II. The lack of funds to support Sunni education was continually cited as one of the causes of the growth of Shi'ism. As late as 1908, Şeyhülislam Mehmed Cemaleddin wrote a report on the continuing problem of Shi'i conversion activities. He maintained that Ottoman confiscation of *evkaf* funds (money from pious endowments) had caused the decline in the quality of Sunni primary schools (Deringil 1990, 56). The loss of the Sunni religious establishment's independent income was as large a factor in the conversion process as Shi'i missionary activity. Sunni religious education was seriously weakened because the government did not invest in building and staffing schools or in producing teaching materials in support of Sunni Islam. The Ottoman government, as a result, could not successfully refute Shi'i propaganda.

Ottoman officials also noted that Shi'i missionary activity was aided by the public performances of passion plays during the yearly *Muharrem*, or *Ashura,* ceremonies. As mentioned earlier, Ottoman tolerance of the ceremonies in the Iraqi provinces had helped spread their popularity, and, by the mid–nineteenth century, public performances were evident not only in Iraq but throughout the empire (Calmard 1989, 176). In 1887, the ceremonies in Istanbul were vividly described in detailed correspondence between the Office of the Grand Vizier and the Ministry of Public Security *(Zabtiye Nezareti):*

> Many groups of Iranians in Istanbul . . . start to mourn on the occasion of the beginning of the month of *Muharrem,* going noisily in the evenings from one house to another. On the Tenth of *Muharrem* from 150 to 200 Persians, wearing white shirts [and with] daggers in their hands, hit their heads and their breasts, drawing blood and with one voice unanimously read the elegy. They organize in the Valide Han and fan out to the other *hans* [commercial caravansaries]. Many foreigners and locals, together with religious students, group in the *hans* and the streets in order to watch them. If the foreigners or locals smile [while watching them], the Persians jeer and a big disaster can be expected. During the day some Ottoman women also look on the spectacle and it is heard that they go inside the *hans.*[19]

The Ottoman government became concerned that the public aspect of these ceremonies would have an adverse effect on the Sunni population and declared in an official memorandum that Iranians should not wander in the streets. Also, Ottoman women were never to enter the *hans,* even in the daytime.[20] The fact that Ottoman women were singled out in the report suggests that officials were also uneasy about issues of public morality. The public nature of the ceremonies was contrary to Ottoman notions of proper public behavior for women, and officials were also worried about the effect these Shi'i observances could have on Sunni women. For security reasons and the protection of public order, the government deemed it necessary to prevent the public performance of these observances, but no evidence has yet appeared suggesting that policing policies were implemented to actually prevent the observances in Istanbul.

19. BOA, Y.A. HUS 207–15, various dates from 5 Muharrem 1305 (23 September 1887) to 11 Muharrem 1305 (29 September 1887). There are many accounts from foreigners of the ceremonies in Istanbul. For a discussion of some of these memoirs, see Glassen 1993, 113–29.

20. BOA, Y.A. HUS 207–15.

The *Muharrem* ceremonies in Baghdad were even more worrisome for the Ottoman government. They were closely connected with the Shi'i program of conversion, which included missionary activity and the awarding of scholarships, medals, and honors to Sunnis who converted to Shi'ism. Aluizade Ahmed Şakir, one of the Iraqi Sunni *ulema,* wrote a report in 1907 that urged the prohibition of passion plays because "they heighten the excitement of the population." More important, he noted, the ceremonies were "much more political than religious" (Deringil 1990, 52). At the time he wrote his report, Iran was in the midst of its Constitutional Revolution (1905–1911) and the observances had assumed a markedly political overtone. Whereas in 1885 the Ottoman government had been concerned with questions of conversion, public order, and moral behavior, twenty years later the observances had also become a vehicle for political opposition that could foster hostilities and create unrest in Iraq. In 1911, a telegram from Baghdad to the Ministry of the Interior warned of the dangers of public performances and passion plays. The Porte decided that, although the ceremonies would not be prevented, they should only be conducted in private. Groups of Iranians were forbidden to parade with their drums *(davuls)* and reed wind instruments *(zurnas)* on the streets of Baghdad either in the daytime or in the evening. The government cited public comfort and security as the reason for limiting the *Muharrem* activities and for moving them out of public spaces.[21]

Sunni Counterpropaganda[22]

Ottoman concerns about conversion were long-standing and became more acute during the reign of Abdülhamid II. Ottoman tolerance of Shi'i rituals, increased Shi'i proselytizing, and the general lack of Ottoman support for Sunni institutions in Iraq fostered the perception that Shi'ism was increasing in the Iraqi provinces. The problem became urgent

21. BOA, Dahiliye Nezareti Siyasi (DH.SYS) 64–35, 27 Kanunuevvel 1326 (9 January 1911).

22. I have borrowed this term from Selim Deringil.

when Abdülhamid attempted to bring Islam to the forefront of his foreign and domestic policies.[23]

Central to Sultan Abdülhamid II's foreign policy was the use of pan-Islam and Muslim unity to counter British, French, Russian, and Dutch interests. Pan-Islamism was a broad movement that sought to transcend political divisions that resulted from foreign incursions, and to mend internal fissures like the Sunni-Shi'i division. The movement was particularly strong in areas such as Russia, India, and China, where Muslim populations had recently come under control of non-Muslim powers. Although the movement may not have aimed to achieve an actual political reunification of all Muslims, it was intended to secure the future of the Muslim world, and that future was to be led by the Ottoman sultan (Yapp 1992, 8).[24]

The caliphate was essential to Abdülhamid's attempt to ensure leadership over the ever-diminishing territories of the empire (Deringil 1993, 21–22). By the time of his ascension to the throne in 1876, many territories had been lost, and many Muslims were now under foreign control. Chris-

23. Of course the secularizing tendencies of the Tanzimat period had not displaced Islamism as a foundation for the reforms. During the reign of the previous three modernizing monarchs—Mahmud II (1808–1839), Abdülmecid (1839–1861) and Abdülaziz (1861–1876)—for example, Ottomanism, which equated loyalty to the dynasty with loyalty to the state, was presented as the basis of state legitimacy. These reformers, however, continued to justify the Tanzimat Reforms in Islamic terms. Intellectuals during the middle decades of the nineteenth century, known as the "Young Ottomans," were nevertheless critical of the secularizing aspects of the reforms of the Tanzimat, accusing the reformers of going too far toward Westernization and neglecting the traditions of Ottoman society. Their intellectual spokesman, Namık Kemal, claimed that the rule of law should be based on Shari'a. They sought to reconcile the Western basis of these reforms with that of Islamic tradition. Although Namık Kemal and the Young Ottomans failed to achieve power in the existing institutions of the state, their focus on Islamic heritage was carried on in the state ideology of pan-Islam during the reign of Sultan Abdülhamid II (see Abu-Manneh 1990, 257–74).

24. Additional studies on the influence of pan-Islamism on Muslims throughout Asia and Africa can be found in Rochlin 1939, 213–21; Reid 1967, 267–83; and Karl 1998, 1096–118.

tian powers, for example, now controlled Muslim populations in Algeria as the result of the French invasion of 1830; the Russians had acquired the khanates in Central Asia at the end of the nineteenth century; the Ottomans had lost Serbia, Rumania, Montenegro, Bosnia and Herzegovina, Cyprus, Egypt, and Tunis; and territory has been ceded to Greece. It was after the loss of the Balkans in the Russian-Ottoman War of 1877–1878 that, early in his regime, Abdülhamid proclaimed an Islamic identity for his regime. He began using the title "Caliph" and also reaffirmed his right to the titles "Protector of the Faithful" *(Emir el-Müminin)* and "Protector of the two Holy Places [Mecca and Medina]" *(Hadim-ül Haremeyn-i Şerifeyn)* (Deringil 1990, 45–62; 1993, 3–29).

While the sultan may not have openly called for a unified Muslim empire—his military power was hardly up to the task of unification—he did, however, use the ideology of pan-Islam and the title of caliph to support his program of strong central authority over eastern Anatolia and the Asian provinces of the empire. He also intended to reestablish a loyalty to Sunni Islam and to the Ottoman dynasty from both Muslims in the empire who had become alienated as the result of the Tanzimat Reforms, and those who now resided in former Ottoman territories (Duguid 1973, 139–55; Farah 1995/1996, 191–212; Buzpinar 1996, 59–89).

The pan-Islamic policy was particularly important for Ottoman-Iranian relations. Under the influence of one of the foremost proponents of pan-Islam, Jamal al-Din al-Afghani, Sultan Abdülhamid undertook a *rapprochement* toward Iran. They considered Sunni-Shi'i unity as a possible long-term solution for the Shi'i problem in Iraq. By 1894, however, Iranian support for Armenian revolutionaries in eastern Anatolia and the sultan's growing dissatisfaction with al-Afghani—who was making secret overtures to the khedive of Egypt—undermined the possibility for improved relations between the two empires.[25]

25. Çetinsaya 2006, 111–12 and 115–16, notes that the Persian newspaper *Akhtar*, which was published in Istanbul from 1876 onward and was known for its pan-Islamic sympathies, was closed by the Porte. This is evidence of Sultan Abdülhamid's later dissatisfaction with the ideology of pan-Islam.

Abdülhamid's support for pan-Islam did not conflict with his belief in the fundamentals of the faith as held by the Hanafi school. In order to reinforce these fundamentals, his government sought to maintain control over the printing and distribution of the Qur'an. The Ottomans produced elaborately illuminated, large-print copies that were given as gifts. This generosity was bestowed on important personages in the provinces as part of a package of incentives to create loyalty in the far-flung territories. In the 1880s, for example, Sanusi sheikhs in the Libyan deserts who were being courted by the Italians were sent Qur'ans to secure tribal loyalty to the empire and aid in transmitting the Ottoman civilizing program to the tribes. A similar policy was followed in the Hijaz and Yemen, where tribal chiefs were "cajoled" with decorations, bribes, and Qur'ans (Deringil 2003, 323, 239–40).

Attempts to control the production of the holy book were not unique to Abdülhamid. In Muslim theology, the Qur'an was revealed in Arabic and the text itself was considered miraculous and inimitable—no human being could replicate the language of the Qu'ran. Jurists were always concerned that textual interpretations, particularly through translations, might mistakenly misinterpret the original meaning or impose an altogether different meaning on the text. Although Muslim theologians and legal scholars differed on the question of whether the Qur'an could be translated, the Hanafi School allowed translation to facilitate prayer for those who did not know Arabic. Abu Hanifa (d. 767), for example, allowed Persian-speakers to recite their prayers in their own language. The Ottomans had a long history, dating back to the thirteenth and fourteenth centuries, of translating the Qur'an into Turkish (Wilson 2009, 420–21).

Considering the centuries-old division between the Ottomans and Iranians, and concerns about the spread of Shi'ism in the Iraqi provinces during the nineteenth century, it is not surprising that the Ottomans would attempt to control the production, publication, and distribution of the Qu'ran in order to counter Shi'i missionary activity. A law of 1276 AH (1859–1860) had strongly forbidden the importation and sale of Qur'ans from Iran and licenses for the right to publish the book were given only to

Sunni-run presses within the Ottoman Empire (Deringil 1993, 23–24).[26] What if, for example, Shi'i *ulema* began to produce copies of the Qur'an that projected their intentions on the text to call for political action against the Ottoman state? Indeed, Ottoman anxiety that it could not control copies of the Qur'an produced outside of the Ottoman center went as far as to include a prohibition of those coming even from Sunni centers in Russia and from al-Azhar in Cairo, the center of Sunni Islam. Muslims in Russia were under the political control of a foreign Christian power, and although Egypt was still a part of the Ottoman Empire, it was self-governing—at least until the British occupation in 1882.

In the 1880s, Iran and Russia protested and petitioned the Ottoman government for removal of the restrictions on publishing and distributing Qur'ans in the Ottoman Empire. In 1885, the Iranian Embassy demanded that the Ottomans issue more licenses. The Ottomans rejected the request and continued to limit publication to Ottoman-Sunni presses. Customs officials were also instructed to confiscate copies of the Qur'an that came from Iran.[27]

This policy continued in the 1890s when Ministry of Education reports reaffirmed the need to prevent Iranian, Russian, and other foreign publishers from printing and distributing copies of the Qur'an. In a report of 1894, the Education Ministry reiterated the need to restrict the publication and distribution of Qur'ans by foreign publishers and continued to call for the limitation of publication to designated Ottoman print-

26. More research needs to be undertaken on Qur'anic interpretation in the late Ottoman and Qajar periods. A very insightful study of Qur'anic interpretations in modern Iran can be found in Amirpur 2005, 337–50. Before the late nineteenth century, Qur'anic interpretation was produced in commentaries written by scholars for other scholars who had detailed knowledge of grammar, law, dogmatics, and the traditions of Muhammad. The great Egyptian thinker Muhammad 'Abduh (1849–1905) considered the Qur'an as inspiration and guidance for a program of an active life. He looked at the holy book as a text that could be understood by the wider public and could have a practical application to daily life (see Baljon 1968, and Jansen 1974).

27. BOA, Meclis-i Vükela (M.V.) 1–19, 18 Rebiyülahir 1302 (4 February 1885).

ing presses. Officials were concerned that foreigners might alter the text because of their lack of knowledge of Arabic and improper placement of vowels, which might corrupt the statutes of Islamic law. Inspectors with the Education Ministry were instructed to investigate cases of illegal copies by foreign printing presses, and were assigned to custom's offices where they were to confiscate Qur'ans being transported into the empire.[28]

In 1896, the Russian consulate intervened in the case of a bookseller in Istanbul named Kerimoff, whose stock of Qur'ans had been confiscated and who was petitioning for compensation. He eventually received compensation for five thousand copies of the Qur'an that he had imported from Russia (Meyer 2007, 23). The following year, in 1897, Muslims from Russia and Iran petitioned for Ottoman approval to print and sell copies of the Qur'an in the Ottoman Empire. Since the printing of the Qur'an had been put under state monopoly, publishers who wanted to produce the holy book had to apply to a newly established state commission for permission; explain the reason why they wanted to print the Qur'an; and show copies to the commission.

The Ottomans' greatest fear was that the text would be changed and these alterations might threaten the stability of the empire. Reasons for these fears could be found in a 1897 memorandum from Minister of Education Zühdü Paşa, to the Office of the Şeyhülislam that was concerned with applications for printing and sale licenses from Russian and Iranian subjects:

> Although it seems inauspicious to forbid the printing of Qur'ans to one who is of the *sunna,* if we open this door it will mean that we will be opening it to any Muslim from Kazan or India or Algeria. . . . This will mean unforeseeable dangers for the Holy Word which has survived untarnished for some thirteen hundred years. Particularly since these are troubled times in which the foreigner's calumnious views regarding

28. BOA, Yıldız Mütenevvi Maruzat (Y.MTV) 89–153, 27 Receb 1311 (3 February 1894); Y.MTV 91–35, 21 Şaban 1311 (27 February 1894).

> the Holy Text multiply. . . . The matter may go well beyond the printing of the Qur'an and, God forbid, create untold complications for the Sublime State. (Deringil 1998, 53)

The restrictions on the printing of Qur'ans continued throughout the reign of Sultan Abdülhamid II. Scholars have suggested that the Ottomans felt threatened by the numerous foreign Muslims who were no longer under Ottoman tutelage and who could, potentially, endanger the legitimacy and authority of the regime (Deringil 1998, 53). This was certainly the case with Shi'i publications of the Qur'an, which the Ottomans felt could be distributed and used as propaganda in the provinces of Iraq.

During the early constitutional period, Ottoman officials continued to monitor the printing and distribution of the Qur'an. In November 1909, Istanbul police raided the business of an Iranian bookbinder in the Valide Han, Mehmed İbrahim Efendi, and discovered and confiscated 1,260 Qur'ans without proper government seals that had been left for binding by a Russian printer, Abbas Efendi. The Iranian Embassy immediately protested the raid, because it was undertaken by two inspectors and numerous police and military officials who had entered Mehmed İbrahim's business illegally and without permission from the consulate. The Embassy deplored the raid and demanded reparations in excess of 12.5 liras for each destroyed copy.[29] The Iranian complaint was based on paragraph three of the Ottoman-Persian Convention of 1875 (see chapter 3), which allowed for protection of Iranian subjects by Iranian consuls and agents, and the intervention of Persian agents in the case of suits or contestations brought against an Iranian by Ottoman authorities (Hertslet 1891, 179–86; Aitchison 1909, 64–66). After investigations, the Foreign Ministry reported that, according to their reading of the first paragraph of the 1875 Convention, it was legal for Ottoman authorities to enter Mehmed İbrahim's business and to confiscate the unlicensed copies of the

29. BOA, DH.MUI 49–2/6, various dates between 4 Zilkade 1327 and 5 Muharrem 1328 (7 November 1909 and 17 January 1910).

Qur'an.[30] The Convention stated that Persian subjects were subject to all of the laws and regulations of the empire in all cases of personal injuries, crimes, and misdemeanors, and were also subject to Ottoman police and tribunals (Hertslet 1891, 179–86; Aitchison 1909, 64–66).

Although reports from Iraq about the growth of Shiʿism and the need for Sunni *ulema* to be sent to the provinces had started reaching Istanbul in the 1820s, it was not until the reign of Abdülhamid II that the Porte began to take extensive measures to counter the expansion of Shiʿism in Iraq (Çetinsaya 2006, 101). In 1885, the Cabinet of Ministers *(Meclis-i Vükela),* the main governing body of the state, held lengthy discussions and declared that it was politically and religiously necessary to halt spread of Shiʿism, particularly in the villages of eastern Anatolia and Iraq. Reports pointed to the ignorance of the principles of Islam among the local tribes as one of the primary reasons for the spread of Shiʿism. The need for proper education in the fundamentals of the Hanafi School was repeatedly cited as the main solution to this problem. The *ulema* were held up for special criticism for their failure to stem the tide of conversion. The Cabinet proposed that trained teachers and religious officials be sent to the Iraqi provinces to teach the virtues of Sunni Islam in primary schools, and that they should be supported by the government so they had sufficient income to live there.[31] A year later, in 1886, Hüsnü Efendi, a tax official who was inspecting real estate in Baghdad and Mosul, returned to Istanbul, and his report on the expansion of Shiʿism prompted the Cabinet, in consultation with the Office of the Şeyhülislam, to declare that mosques and schools should be founded immediately in Baghdad to promote Sunni belief and prevent the further expansion of Shiʿism.[32]

In 1892, as a part of the Ottoman centralization program that was intended to foster a loyal population in the peripheries, the government opened an imperial school for tribes *(aşiret mektebi)* in Istanbul. One of

30. BOA, DH.MUI 49–2/6, 5 Muharrem 1328 (17 January 1910).

31. BOA, M.V. 1–26, 22 Rebiyülahir 1302 (8 February 1885). See also Deringil 1990, 30.

32. BOA, M.V. 12–53, 20 Cemaziyülevvel 1303 (24 February 1886).

the goals of this school was to introduce these students to the modern world. In the Ottoman imperial view, the tribes were backward and ignorant and lived outside the reach of the Ottoman modernization program. Tribes were also a natural oppositional force to centralization; they were often autonomous and essentially acted as an independent governing system in areas outside of central control. Their political and legal authority, for example, extended to the collection of taxes and administration of justice (Rogan 1996, 84). In the first year of its operation, the tribal school included students from the Arab provinces of Trablusgarb, Bingazi, Haleb, Zor, Hama, Şam, Kudüs-i Şerif, Hijaz, Yemen, Baghdad, and Basra. Kurdish students were recruited from Bitlis, Van, Ma'muretül'aziz, Erzurum, and Diyarbekir. Of the eighty-eight original students, four were from Baghdad and eight were from Basra (Rogan 1996, 88–90). This five-year program included a rigorous curriculum that grounded the students in the basics of Arabic, Ottoman Turkish, French, and Persian, as well as the Qur'an, theology, calligraphy, lexicology, and Islamic and Ottoman history. The sciences were an essential part of the educational program and included geography, engineering, and accounting. Forty-five of the original eighty-eight students who graduated were directed to higher education in the military or civil service academies *(Mekteb-i Harbiye* and the *Mekteb-i Mülkiye),* after which they entered state service. This experiment ended in 1907, and recent scholarship suggests that recruitment was difficult because provincial authorities found it nearly impossible to persuade tribal leaders to send their children to Istanbul. Those who did attend, however, successfully graduated and moved into middle-level civil and military service. Many had long careers that lasted until the end of the empire, suggesting that the goal of creating loyal citizens out of tribesmen was somewhat successful (Rogan 1996, 96–103).

In 1890, the governor of Basra sent a report to the Cabinet concerning conversion in the villages and among nomadic tribes who came from Iran for cultivation or in order to escape from military service. He claimed that three out of four people in the region were inclined toward Shi'ism because "Iranian *ulema* spread Shi'ism to every village and tribe, designating the Arab Shi'a as 'believers'" once they had converted. Iran supported the converts by as much as five or six *kuruş* per year. The governor claimed that the Iranian tribes were proud of their devotion to Allah and actually preferred Ottoman citizenship because of the "great oppression of the people in Iran," and "in order to be free from the interference of the Iranian government." In order to stop the spread of Shi'ism, the governor outlined a number of steps, going as far as to suggest the exile of all religious officials who "lead others to follow the path of ignorance." He also suggested that leaders and sheikhs of tribes be enticed into the Sunni camp with decorations of appreciation. Imams should be appointed who were aware of the conditions in Iraq, who knew the Arabic language, the Qur'an, and tribal life, and who were loyal to the state. These imams were to establish tribal schools, receive a salary, and "protect the children from ignorance and teach the principles of religion."[33]

Grand Vizier Kamil Paşa issued a memorandum in 1891 in support of the education and training of *ulema*. He suggested that Shi'i students from Iraq be sent to al-Azhar under government sponsorship where they would be educated for eight to ten years in the fundamentals of Arabic and the basics of Sunni law. The goal was to return the graduates to their homes to teach in local schools. His proposals were based on his observations of American Protestant missionary schools, which taught Armenians and then sent them back to proselytize in their homeland. Since Egypt was under British influence, the sultan decided to send the students to Istanbul instead (Çetinsaya 2006, 106–7). Thirteen Shi'i and two Sunni students were enrolled in the Valide *medrese* in Istanbul in February 1893. It was hoped that these students would abandon their loyalty to their tribes and to Shi'ism and learn respect for their country and for the Hanafi School.[34] By June, however, twelve of the students had requested travel expenses to return home. The three students who remained were employed after graduation to teach in the mosques and schools, to settle among the Shi'i population, to advise refugees, and to bring the "true path" to the people.[35] Because of the low graduation rate,

33. BOA, Y.MTV 43–117, 4 Haziran 1306 (16 June 1890).
34. BOA, Y.MTV 74–133, 29 Receb 1310 (16 February 1893).
35. BOA, Y.MTV 78–158, 20 Zilkade 1310 (5 June 1893).

this program was considered a failure, and there is no evidence that it continued to operate after that time.

No serious military action was ever considered as a solution to the problem of conversion of the Sunni population to Shi'ism. Education of the population and training of the *ulema* were continually cited as the proper solutions for the problem. Emphasis on proper education during the Hamidian period was a part of larger centralization efforts in the eastern provinces and seen as the most effective means for social engineering projects such as bringing the true faith to marginal communities, and creating a population loyal to the empire (Fortna 2002, 63–66, 93–95, 241–47). As a response to Shi'i propaganda materials that were circulating, Süleyman Hüsnü Paşa, the governor of Baghdad, suggested in an 1892 memorandum that the state prepare a "Book of Beliefs" *(kitab ul-akaid)* that would counter, point-by-point, the false doctrine of the Shi'a and other heretical sects. He noted that a minority of the population now followed Sunni Islam, and Shi'i missionary activity was the primary cause. This book would be a manual for the *ulema* who were assigned to go into the countryside and actively proselytize like the Christian missionaries *(Dai-ul-hak Misyoner)* (Deringil 1993, 18–19; 1998, 49, 133).

Outside of educational reforms, a former Şeyhülislam, Hüseyn Hüsnü Efendi, suggested the creation of a type of "religious secret service" composed of Sunni *ulema* whose job would be to monitor Shi'i activities in the region and inform the Porte.[36] Other reports suggested that the Ottomans should pay more attention to the upkeep of the shrines at Karbala' and Najaf, which were being maintained by large donations from the Iranian government and from Shi'i pilgrimage traffic. Ottoman control over the shrine cities and over the movements of Iranian pilgrims was considered essential for curbing the expansion of Shi'ism among the population (Deringil 1990, 51–52).

The Ottomans were not only worried about conversion but also about sectarian tensions that might be inflamed by British and Russian interests

36. Selim Deringil 1990, coined the term "religious secret service," 50.

in the Iraqi provinces.[37] By the end of the nineteenth century, Iraq and the Persian Gulf had become a territory of economic and military interest as the British tried to protect and expand trade routes to their Indian colonies. At the same time, the Russians were attempting to establish warm-water ports in the Gulf. The provinces were no longer merely territories contested by Ottomans and Iranians, they were also the centers of an international political struggle for economic supremacy. On occasion this struggle manifested in conflicts between Sunnis and Shi'is that the Ottomans suspected were inflamed by the rivalries of the great powers.

A conflict broke out in Samarra' in 1886 when a Sunni *mufti* caused an outrage by reportedly cursing the Shi'i population of the town. Both Shi'ites and Sunnis accused each other of provocations. When the Iranian government asked for the deportation of the accused officials, the Ottoman government called for an investigation to be led by Grand Vizier Kamil Paşa, which dragged on for months. (Çetinsaya 2006, 102–3). Problems between Shi'ites and Sunnis in Samarra' had more serious international consequences when another serious incident occurred in 1893. The episode initially began as a dispute over money on credit between Sunni and Shi'i residents, then escalated to murder and rioting. Many people were wounded, and one Iranian was killed. Shi'i *mujtahids* allegedly incited the population by calling for the closure of stores and by refusing to conduct the Friday prayers. The incident became an international event that involved not only the Iranian government but also the British and Russian governments.[38] International rivalry may have been at the heart of the 1893 incident in Samarra'. Ottoman officials maintained that the Shi'i *mujtahid,* Mirza Hasan Şirazi, was in fact an agent for the

37. From as early as the 1830s British agents had begun staking out influence in the region. By 1840 they had gained control over much of the wealth of the Oudh bequest that contributed to the upkeep of the Shi'i shrine cities (see Cole 1986, 469, 472, and 475; also Çetinsaya 2006, 100). For a detailed discussion of the international contest over Iraq, see Farah 1996, 175–90.

38. BOA, Y.A.HUS 296–39, 4 Cemaziyülahir 1311 (18 December 1893); Y.A. HUS 299–27, 7 Zilhicce 1311 (11 June 1894); M.V. 80–65, 26 Zihicce 1312 (20 June 1895). For a detailed discussion of this affair, see Çetinsaya 2006, 112–14.

British. The British asked for permission from the Porte to send a steamship to Samarra' in order to protect British students residing there. The Dragoman of the Russian Consulate, however, claimed that the British wanted to send a steamship to aid Mirza Hasan Şirazi's escape to India. The Ottoman government rejected the British request because moving warships on the internal rivers of the empire was a violation of existing treaties. They called for an investigation into the matter and the arrest of those involved in the incident. In the end, an assistant business manager *(karperdaz),* Mirza Paşa was arrested for his involvement. Three Iranian *ulema* from Najaf were also accused of calling for the closing of stores in Samarra' and for not conducting Friday prayers. The Ottoman government banished the Iranians who had been involved in this event, including the Iranian Assistant Consul *(Şehbender-i Vekili)* in Samarra', who was believed not only to have provoked the disturbance but also to have caused the death of one of the participants.[39]

By calling for investigations and taking action against the various agents and participants in the disputes in Samarra', Abdülhamid hoped to calm the situation. His actions, however, were insufficient. In 1894, a telegraph from Shi'i notables in Baghdad reached the Porte along with a petition containing 270 signatures complaining that certain Sunni imams were threatening and insulting the Shi'a and provoking conflicts between the Sunni and Shi'i population. After an official investigation, the complaints of the Shi'a were found to be true. The Sunni imams were charged with causing serious disputes between the populations. Sixth Army Field Marshall Receb Paşa had also apparently encouraged the provocation. The investigators recommended that they be replaced.[40]

By 1905, the Shi'i 'problem' in Iraq took on a new dimension when the Shi'i *ulema* in the shrine cities became politically divided into pro- and anticonstitutionalists during the Constitutional Revolution in Iran.

39. BOA, Y.A.HUS 296–39, 4 Cemaziyülahir 1311 (18 December 1893); Y.A. HUS 299–27, 7 Zilhicce 1311 (11 June 1894); M.V. 80–65, 26 Zihicce 1312 (20 June 1895).

40. BOA, Y.A.HUS 299–27, 2 Zilhicce 1311 (6 June 1894); also M.V. 80–65, 26 Zilhicce 1312 (20 June 1895).

In this period the Porte again attempted to assert some central control over the region by undertaking new reforms. More teachers were sent to southern Iraq to spread the Sunni creed. The Ottoman government also recognized that poverty was a major reason for the increase in conversion to Shiʿism and called for more development projects, especially irrigation works.

The issue of conversion in the nineteenth and early twentieth century was a matter directly connected to the geopolitical realities of the period as well as Ottoman centralizing policies in the Iraqi frontier provinces. In the early part of the nineteenth century, the Ottoman Empire needed to reassert direct control over the provinces to increase agriculture and tax revenues as it entered the world market. By the end of the century, the provinces had become cornerstones of international politics where the British and Russians fought for influence in the region while the Ottomans attempted to keep control over its distant provinces. Throughout the century, Shiʿi conversion and the population's potential disloyalty became the Ottoman administration's central focus. Within the context of the geopolitical rivalries in the Iraqi provinces and domestic concerns, the Ottomans renewed and reasserted their interest in prohibiting marriage between Ottomans and Iranians. Since most of these marriages occurred in Iraq, conversion was of particular concern because the Ottomans believed that Ottoman-Iranian marriages would lead to an increase in the Shiʿi population. The ban on Sunni-Shiʿi marriages, therefore, was part of this effort to forestall further conversions (Çetinsaya 2006, 117–26).

3

From Subjecthood to Citizenship

THE OTTOMAN CONCEPT of citizenship developed within the framework of an "official nationalism," which attempted to create a "willed merger of nation and dynastic empire."[1] By the 1860s, reformers began to promote the imperial ideology of Ottomanism *(Osmanlılık)* to try to strengthen the state's legitimacy and maintain the loyalty of all of its subjects, even as the empire rapidly disintegrated, territorially. As an imperial ideology, Ottomanism became the ideological basis for the long (and uneven) conferral of rights and responsibilities of citizenship.

The most important definition of citizenship was detailed in the Law of Ottoman Nationality *(Tabi'iyet-i Osmaniye Kanunnamesi)*, enacted on 3 January 1869 (Ahmad 1984, 53–64).[2] The nationality law was a part of the centralizing policies of the Tanzimat that designated who were legal residents and who were foreigners on the basis of residence and birth (Saltzmann 1999, 45; and see appendix B, this book). The law was enacted only five years before Ottoman officials began to refocus on the importance of marriage demographics and to revisit the prohibition of marriage between Ottomans and Iranians. When they addressed the marriage prohibition in 1874, officials were primarily concerned with marriage in the eastern provinces of Iraq.

The 7 October 1874 Law Protecting the Prohibition of Marriage Between Iranians and Ottoman Citizens

On 7 October 1874, the Ottomans enacted the Law Protecting the Prohibition of Marriage Between Iranians and Ottoman Citizens *(Tebaa-i*

1. Seton-Watson 1977, chapters 4 and 6; Anderson 1994, chapter 6, particularly p. 86.

2. See also Kuran 1968, 109–17; Makdisi 2002b, 29–48.

Devlet-i Aliyye ile tebaa-i İraniyenin izdivacı haklarında olan memnuiyetin muhafazasına dair nizamnamedir). This law most clearly reflected the intersection of the demographic importance of marriage and geopolitical exigencies in the frontier provinces of Iraq.[3] It contained three articles:

> 1. Marriages between Ottoman and Iranian citizens, as in olden times, are strongly prohibited.
>
> 2. Those [officials] who are authorized to perform marriages and who act against the prohibition will be held responsible.
>
> 3. [If] a woman who is an Ottoman citizen marries someone who is an Iranian citizen against the prohibition, both the woman and her children will be considered Ottoman citizens and liable for conscription, military tax, and all other financial obligations.[4]

This law established the only exception to the universally accepted international legal standard of "dependent citizenship" provided for in Article 7 of the 1869 Law of Ottoman Nationality. The principle of dependent citizenship held that in the case of a marriage of mixed nationalities, the married woman would lose her birth citizenship (marital expatriation) and acquire the citizenship of her husband (marital naturalization).[5]

3. BOA, Yıldız Resmi Maruzat (Y.A.RES) 37–8, 25 Shaban 1291 (7 October 1874). The law can also be found in draft form in the *Ecnebi Defterleri* 43/1, s. 17–18, which includes discussions that took place in the Meclis-i Vükela, and can be found in final form in the *Düstur* 1. tertip, 4. cilt, s. 614. See appendix C.

4. No evidence has come to light suggesting that the Ottoman government was actively concerned with these marriages between 1822 and 1874.

5. "Tabi'iyet-i Osmaniye Kanunnamesi," *Düstur,* 1. tertip, 1. cilt, s. 16–18. The additions to this law are found in *Takvim-i Velayi,* no. 1044, 10 Şevval 1285 (14 January 1869). On the subject of dependent citizenship from the beginning of the twentieth century, see Waltz 1937, 13–15. There is also an expanding body of literature on the intersection of gender, marriage, and citizenship (see Wildenthal 2001 and Heuer 2005). On use of the terms *marital expatriation* and *naturalization,* see Bredbenner 1998 and Augustine-Adams 2002, 8–30. Augustine-Adams examines how the Argentine Supreme Court, which had no civil law of dependent citizenship, divided a married

Under Article 7, an Ottoman woman would, thereby, acquire the citizenship of her foreign husband. The article stated, however, that a woman who married a foreigner while she was an Ottoman subject could reclaim her original nationality if she petitioned for it within three years of her husband's death. The provision of this article applied to the person. The matter of ownership of *mülk* and *arazi* property was subject to general laws and regulations. The 1874 prohibition was in direct contradiction to the nationality law. In the 1874 prohibition, an Ottoman woman who married an Iranian man would not forfeit her citizenship and acquire the Iranian citizenship of her husband. She and her children would, instead, continue to be counted as Ottoman citizens.

It is important not to underestimate the fundamentally gendered nature of dependent citizenship as upheld in the Law of Ottoman Nationality of 1869 and in the 1874 prohibition. The 1869 nationality law was modeled on a French law of 7 February 1851 that was itself based on the 1804 French Civil Code, also known as the Napoleonic Code. Articles 12 and 19 of the Napoleonic Code addressed the issue of dependent citizenship in stating, respectively, that "the foreigner who shall have married a Frenchman shall follow the condition of her husband," and "a Frenchwoman who shall espouse a foreigner shall follow the condition of her husband."[6] The basis underlying this system of dependent citizenship was a model of patriarchal authority stemming from ancient Roman tradition, by which the father had all rights as the head of the family *(pater potestas)*. French law considered the woman to be a legal minor who was required to obey her husband in return for his protection and support. When the

woman's citizenship, making her both dependent and independent of her husband's citizenship, while nevertheless upholding the principle of dependent citizenship with the reasoning that a women "implicitly consents" to take her husband's citizenship when she agrees to marry him.

6. For reference to the French law of 7 February 1851, see Plender 1974, 709–47, and Aybay 1980, 63; for the French Civil Code of 1804, see Thao 1929, 63, and Camiscioli 1999, 54–55.

Ottomans adopted French law in 1869 as the Law of Ottoman Nationality , they strengthened the existing patriarchal structures of the Ottoman family whereby the husband maintained final authority over his household. It is important to note, however, that under Islamic law, women had more property rights than European women because the husband and wife did not merge their property but held it separately. This was particularly the case in cities and urban societies where women had more access to the courts and could assert their rights. Administrative law *(kanun)* regulated property rights in rural, agricultural, and nomadic societies where patriarchal structures allowed for stronger male control over property. The gender structures of Ottoman society nevertheless reinforced and supported the new ruling strategies concerning citizenship, thereby legitimizing those foreign patrimonial sources of power.

In 1874, the legislators stressed the need for a clear and final decision on the matter of marriage between Ottomans and Iranians. It will be seen, however, that over the course of the following decades, the law would create more confusion than clarity. Discussions that took place in the Cabinet *(Meclis-i Vükela)* when the law was drafted stressed that this prohibition had been in force since "olden times." They referred to the 1822 Supreme Mandate of Sultan Mahmud II and the language of religious and sectarian division, appealing to an authority that harked back to past Sunni-Shi'i conflicts. Beyond the religious rhetoric, the 1874 law was also framed within the context of nationalities. Marriages between Ottomans and Iranians were forbidden on the basis of citizenship *(tabi'iyet),* which clearly indicated that the connection between marriage and citizenship was essential to the Ottoman program of centralization and the creation of a loyal population in the frontier provinces of Iraq.

The Law of Ottoman Nationality of 1869 and the 1874 prohibition accepted the standard of dependent citizenship that denied women their own choice of husbands. In accepting that women would lose their citizenship upon marriage, the Ottomans subjected women's citizenship rights to the requirements of geopolitical concerns. The importance of demographics to these marriages and its relationship to Ottoman concerns about its frontiers can clearly be seen when we examine two other cases in which the government considered exceptions to the 1869 Law of Ottoman

Nationality. In 1889, the legal advisers to the Ministry of the Interior discussed the matter of Algerian Muslims carrying French passports who were seeking asylum in the Ottoman Empire. The Ottomans lost Algeria to the French in 1830, when they began the process of turning the territory into a settler colony. The French confiscated much of the most productive land in Muslim hands through various processes, including *cantonnement,* whereby tribes were forced to relinquish this land for the purpose of European colonization. French policies to create a settler colony met with militant resistance. In the final decade of his reign, Napoléon III (1848–1870) ended the practice of *cantonnement* and endorsed a policy of political assimilation of Muslims and Jews, which would allow voluntary adoption of French citizenship. Article 1 of the Senate Decree on the Naturalization of Muslims and Jews in Algeria and the Public Administrative Regulation for its Execution, 14 July 1865–21 April 1866 stated that upon application a Muslim or Jewish Algerian could "be granted the rights of French citizenship [and] in this case, he shall be governed under the civil and political laws of France" (Hurewitz 1975, 1:355–59). In fact, very few Muslims chose to adopt French citizenship. In 1870, four years after the decree was enacted, only 194 Algerians had applied for French citizenship. By 1890, only one year after the Ottomans were considering the status of Algerian Muslims carrying French passports, only 736 had applied for French citizenship. By 1906, only 1,362 Muslims had made this choice (Hurewitz 1975, 1:355–59).

Despite the fact the very few Algerian Muslims chose French citizenship, some of them came to the attention of the legal advisors to the Ministry of the Interior. The Porte issued a decree on 20 November 1889 that gave these Algerians two years after their arrival to decide whether to remain French citizens and leave the Ottoman state, or become Ottoman citizens and be allowed to establish permanent residence. As French citizens they would be prohibited from marrying Ottoman women. If they contravened this prohibition, they were to be treated the same as Iranians and sent into exile (Deringil 1993, 24–25, and 1998, 55–56). The decision to extend the prohibition to Algerians was a singular case and valid only for Algerians who refused to give up their French citizenship. The very fact that Algerians could give up their passports highlights a major difference between Algerians and Iranians. At the time of the 1889 decree, Algeria had not been a province of the Ottoman Empire for fifty-nine years, and it was also no longer frontier territory. Algerians were also Sunnis and former subjects of the Ottoman Empire and, therefore, had a different status from that of the Iranian Shi'a who were viewed as "foreign nationals." Algerians were given the opportunity to relinquish their French passports for the privilege of becoming Ottoman citizens. There is no evidence that Iranians were offered the option of relinquishing their passports and becoming Ottoman citizens. To date, scholarship does not exist on the connection between passports and citizenship rights, and further research is needed to understand the mechanisms by which passports allowed government control over immigration in ways that differed from the lack of such control in frontier regions where borders were more porous.

The second case occurred much later, in 1917, and concerned the large numbers of Ottoman women who were married to Greek nationals and, as a consequence, had assumed their husbands' Greek citizenship. The matter was considered within the broader context of a revisitation of the question of the citizenship of Ottomans who married foreign citizens. Legal advisors to the Interior Ministry stated, "The unity of the family assures the political unity of the state," and that, in the case of marriages of mixed nationalities, the citizenship laws of most civilized states determined that the marriage affects the citizenship of the wife.[7] If a foreign woman (a woman who was not an Ottoman citizen) married an Ottoman man, she was considered an Ottoman citizen, and if an Ottoman woman married a foreigner (a man who was not an Ottoman citizen), she acquired the citizenship of her husband. The legal advisors commented that the Ottoman citizenship law was "based on the goal of the equality of the spouses," and when the wife acquired the citizenship of her husband, the children born from them would be Ottoman citizens and there was no "injury to the government."[8] The legal advisers cautioned, however, that great harm

7. BOA, Dahiliye Nezareti Hukuk Müşavirliği (DH.HMŞ) 1–1/8–5, 4 Temmuz 1333 (4 July 1917).

8. Ibid.

would come to the state because of the large numbers of Ottoman women and their children and grandchildren who had already acquired Greek citizenship. When considering extending the prohibition of Ottoman-Iranian marriages to Ottoman-Greek marriages, in which case the wives and children would have been considered Ottoman citizens, the legal advisers upheld Article 7 of the 1869 Law of Ottoman Nationality and deemed it unsuitable "for political reasons" to prohibit these marriages. They reasoned that "marriages between Ottoman women and foreigners are legal, and the law is just."[9] There were significant differences between the Greek and Iranian cases. Like the Algerians, the Greeks carried passports that were subject to inspection by Ottoman authorities, who maintained records and controlled their immigration. The Greek border was a frontier closer to the center of Ottoman power and not subject to the difficulties of direct rule that confronted the Ottomans in the more distant provinces of Iraq. An ethnically Greek population had existed in the Ottoman Empire since its creation. Iranians were more recent settlers in the eastern Iraqi provinces, particularly in the Shi'i shrine cities, or they were part of the seasonal tribal migrations between the Ottoman and Iranian states that were difficult to control. Iranians certainly carried passports, which the Iranian government had begun issuing as early as 1853. But Iranians in the empire tended to maintain their Iranian citizenship. The Shi'i *ulema* in the shrine cities of Najaf and Karbala', for example, maintained their Iranian citizenship.[10]

The 1869 Law of Ottoman Nationality and the 1874 Law Protecting the Prohibition of Marriage Between Iranians and Ottoman Citizens, as well as subsequent decrees discussed below, show increasing government involvement in the minutiae of Ottoman life. Such penetration into daily life, a product of modernizing states throughout the world and not unique to the Ottomans, was, nevertheless, very much a feature of Abdülhamid's

9. Ibid.

10. The Majlis did not ratify the first Iranian citizenship law until 1929. Iranian rules on citizenship were subsequently collected in volume 2 of the Civil Code of 1934 (see Yeganeh 1992, 634–35).

policies (Deringil 1998, 18).[11] Throughout the years of the Hamidian regime until the end of the empire, the prohibition of marriages with Iranians was reconfirmed and reinforced on the basis of contemporary expediencies and geopolitical concerns. Yet the original basis of the prohibition—the Shi'i-Sunni religious difference—was continually invoked to support the continuation of the prohibition. On 12 June 1914, for example, officials in the Office of the Şeyhülislam and legal advisors to the Ministry of the Interior discussed if marriage contracts between Sunnis and "heretics"—whether Mu'tezile, Shi'i, or Caferi—who followed doctrines that questioned the articles of faith, were contrary to the Shari'a. In considering this matter, the legal advisors sent the following response upholding the reasons for the original prohibition and for its continuation:

> Since ancient times marriages between Ottoman Muslim women and Iranians were prohibited, even as far back as [the time of] Yavuz Sultan Selim I because of the political system in use in the Ottoman State [at that time].
>
> The *ferman* dated 11 Rebiyülahir 1237 (5 January 1822) of Sultan Mahmud II states, "As a result of the marriage with Iranians and persons of unknown lineage who are inclined to Shi'ism, [and] Rafızı *mezheps,* the *ferman* was issued, one by one, to the *kadıs* in İstanbul, Eyüp and Üsküdar and to the neighborhood imams. Those imams who contract the marriages and those who give [their daughters] to these persons of unknown lineage will be liable for serious punishment, so that these [marriages] will not occur after this time.
>
> After the Tanzimat the [need for] the prevention [of these marriages] was understood since many Ottoman women, especially in Iraq

11. It should also be noted that government penetration into the daily life of its subjects was not only a part of the modernization process, but was also a characteristic of the imperialist project of conquest and centralization. Leslie Peirce 2003, clearly shows this process of official penetration in her examination of Aintab court records from 1540–1541, a period when the Ottomans had only one generation earlier conquered the region from the Mamluks, and where officials were intimately involved in local matters in order to Ottomanize the region.

> and some other districts, married Iranians in order to release their sons from military service. The system of conscription of male children who are born as a result of these marriages between *mezheps* was adopted. . . .
>
> The *nizamname* dated 27 Şaban 1291/24 Eylül 1290 [7 October 1874] strengthening the aforesaid prohibition was enacted.[12]

The legal advisors referred to Article 3 of the 1874 law and determined that the regulations of the law were clear, and, in the case of these marriages, both the women and their children were counted as Ottoman citizens. The male children were liable for military service, and the wives and children were subject to all other tax obligations of citizenship. The advisors, in addition, concluded that the prohibition should continue because there were 100,000 Iranians living in the empire and, if they marry as they so chose, there would be thousands of children who would be foreigners in the empire.

The Capitulatory Regime and the Ottoman-Persian Convention of 1875

By the 1860s, the Ottoman government recognized that the capitulatory regime on the whole was having serious ramifications for Ottoman control over its subjects. Ottoman concessions allowing foreign powers to protect their own subjects in the empire had reached such levels of abuse that a significant percentage of non-Muslim Ottoman subjects were under the protection of foreign states. This was most apparent in the case of the Russians, who were interfering in the affairs of the empire through their Orthodox subjects. The bilateral Ottoman-Russian Treaty of Kuçuk Kaynarca in 1774 was a watershed in redefining relations between the Ottomans and foreign states that held capitulatory rights. From the earliest years of the empire, the Ottomans had considered that the capitulations and privileges granted to foreign powers could be abrogated at the

12. BOA, Hukuk Muşavirliği İstişare Odası (HR.HMŞ.İSO) 7–1/1, 2 Teşrinisani 1331 (15 November 1915).

will of the sultan. When the Ottomans began to enter into bilateral treaties, the capitulations took on the status of legal agreements that were no longer privileges but were obligations. This led to a loss of Ottoman authority over foreigners who were subjects of states with capitulatory rights, and an increase in interference by foreign powers in the Ottoman Empire. Ottoman subjects could receive protected status, or appointments known as *berats,* which would place them outside of Ottoman law. The Russians were particularly active in selling such appointments and claiming the right to protect Ottoman Orthodox subjects. By 1808, an estimated 120,000 people in the Ottoman Empire were under Russian protection (Ahmad 2000, 1–5).

The Ottoman Tanzimat reformers initially believed that the capitulations brought needed economic benefit to the empire. But by the time of the Paris peace conference in 1856 (that ended the Crimean War), 'Ali Paşa, the grand vizier, noted that the Ottoman Empire was an equal partner with European states and, therefore, since the capitulations were not agreements between partners of equal status, they should be abolished. European powers forestalled discussion of the abolition of the capitulatory system and postponed it for a later convention, which never occurred. In the 1850s and 1860s, the Ottomans viewed the capitulations as a sign of inferiority and made various proposals to European nations to rectify this problem. 'Ali Paşa especially wished to stop abuses by foreigners and Ottoman subjects under foreign protection who did not pay taxes and could not be subject to Ottoman law and justice (Ahmad 2000, 6–7). But no permanent solution was found to the inequities of the system.

The Iranian government had been accorded a measure of capitulatory rights during the reign of Sultan Mahmud II. During the succeeding decades, the Iranians continued to demand the same privileges for their subjects in the empire as were accorded to European communities. The Ottomans, however, delayed conferring on the Iranians the same capitulatory status as other European powers, out of fear that they would also abuse the system. It is reasonable to assume that the Ottomans were particularly concerned that the Iranians might offer protective status to Ottoman citizens of Iranian origin. The Ottomans' consideration of Iranian capitulatory status may well have been a motivating factor in revisiting the 1822 prohibition of marriage between Ottomans and Iranians and enacting a new law in 1874.

Fuller capitulatory rights were, however, finally confirmed for the Iranians in the Ottoman-Persian Convention of 20 December 1875, a reciprocal treaty that granted the same privileges to Ottomans residing in the Iranian state as to Iranians living in Ottoman territory. The Convention reconfirmed that Iranian consuls had the same rights as their European counterparts. Article 4 stated that consuls and vice-consuls of Persia residing in Ottoman territory were charged to look after the security and protection of the interests of their nationals who were traveling or residing in the empire (Aitchison 1909, lxiv–lxv; Nakash 1994, 17–18).[13] In 1885, the Iranian government requested the right to appoint additional consuls for the protection of its citizens in smaller towns in Iraq. The Ottoman government rejected this request on the basis that there were no Iranian citizens in the towns mentioned, and Iranian consuls in the major cities could sufficiently handle the needs of Iranian citizens in the region. The Ottomans, however, permitted Iran to appoint consuls for the needs of Iranian traders and pilgrims traveling to and from Mecca, Medina, and Erzurum, and the pilgrimage sites in Iraq, as had been approved under the 1875 Convention.[14] Litigation between Iranians was now to be settled by Iranian consuls *(şehbenders)* and their assistants. Court cases concerning civil and criminal matters involving Ottomans and Iranians were no longer under the jurisdiction of the Shari'a courts but were transferred to mixed tribunals, where consular representatives could offer protection and assistance in the judicial proceedings. Matters of personal status between Muslim and non-Muslim Ottoman and Iranian citizens were, however, still under the jurisdiction of the Shari'a courts (Aitchison 1909, lxiv–lxv).

13. Yitzhak Nakash, in his seminal study of the Shi'a in Iraq, maintains that the Ottomans gave capitulatory rights to Iran because they could not control their eastern provinces and did not want to go to war over the status of Iranians in Iraq. Nakash points out that, although Iran was probably not able to militarily threaten Istanbul itself, it did wield tremendous power regionally—enough power to force the Ottomans to grant these capitulatory rights.

14. BOA, M.V. 1–19, 18 Rebiyülahir 1302 (4 February 1885).

The Ottoman government's recognition of the territoriality of law as existing alongside the personality of law, which is evinced in the 1875 Ottoman-Persian Convention, increased government intervention in the personal affairs of its subjects. The impact of the Convention on Ottoman intervention in the domestic affairs of its citizens was clearly evident in disputes that arose between non-Muslim subjects. Before the Convention of 1875, cases of personal status between members of Christian and Jewish-Ottoman citizens and non-Ottoman Christians and Jews who resided in the empire were handled within the jurisdiction of the religious courts.[15] While the Convention did not fundamentally change Ottoman agreements with these communities, the recognition of the territoriality of law raised conflicts over questions of jurisdiction. In 1910, the Greek Orthodox Patriarchate in Bursa was involved in a jurisdictional dispute with an Iranian *karperdaz* concerning a case of support *(nafaka)* between two Greek Orthodox-Iranian citizens, one Petroaliseleksi and his wife, Manya. The legal advisors to the Office of the Grand Vizier were asked to decide who had the authority to rule in this case. The advisors referred to Article 1 of the 1875 Convention whereby all cases between Iranian citizens were to be settled by their own consuls, and further noted that agreements with the non-Muslim religious communities *(millets)* concerned only matters between Ottoman citizens. The Bursa diocese, therefore, had no jurisdiction over this case.[16]

Similar problems arose concerning non-Muslim Ottoman citizens residing in Iran. In 1910, the legal advisory council to the Office of the Ottoman Grand Vizier was asked for a ruling on the divorce case of Sedrak Hartunyan, an Ottoman-Armenian citizen who lived in Tebriz. The advisors cited Article 7 of the 1875 convention, which stated:

> all cases and litigation arising between Iranian citizens will be settled by the Iranian consuls or consular assistants . . . [and] final settlements,

15. See Hurewitz 1975, 315–18 for a translation of the *Islahat Fermanı* (18 February 1856) reaffirming the privileges of non-Muslim communities.

16. BOA, DH.MUİ 128–12, 28 Ağustos 1326 (7 September 1910); see also HR.HMŞ.İŞO 7–1/1, 31 Ağustos 1326 (13 September 1910).

> prescriptions for punishments and other procedures will be under [their] jurisdiction.[17]

The advisors went on to cite Article 10 of the Convention, which stated:

> reciprocal procedures concerning Ottoman citizens found in Iran will be carried out.[18]

The divorce case of Sedrak Hartunyan, therefore, was under the jurisdiction of Ottoman officials. The legal advisors recommended that a committee be formed, composed of three Ottoman citizens who resided in Tebriz, including the Ottoman consul and one priest from the Ottoman-Armenian community.

In that same year the more complicated divorce case of Ohannes Ohannesyan and his wife, both of whom were Ottoman-Armenian citizens living in Tebriz, was presented to the legal advisory committee. At issue was the jurisdiction of non-Ottoman-Armenian religious officials. Ohannes Ohannesyan had requested a settlement of his divorce case from the Armenian Patriarchate in Azerbaijan. The advisors again cited the 1875 Convention, which authorized Iranian representatives to examine cases between Iranians who lived in the Ottoman state and Ottoman representatives to examine cases involving Ottomans who live in Iran. The advisors confirmed that the examination of marriage and divorce cases of non-Muslims was for the religious authorities of the sect. They found, however, that a ruling by the Patriarchate in Azerbaijan would infringe on the jurisdiction of Ottoman officials. The case was to be examined by Ottoman religious officials. The Ottoman Consul (*Şehbender)* was neither authorized nor competent to adjudicate divorce cases between non-Muslim Ottoman citizens; therefore, the jurisdiction of such cases belonged to the priests of the Patriarchate. The advisors did recognize that most Ottoman citizens living in Iran would find it financially difficult to travel to Ottoman territory to seek legal advice

17. BOA, HR.HMŞ.İŞO 7–1/1, 31 Ağustos 1326 (13 September 1910).
18. Ibid.

from the nearest religious authority of their sect. On the other hand, if Ottoman citizens applied to the local religious authorities in Iran, they would be subject to the "dangers" of Iranian jurisdiction. As a solution, the legal advisers required that Ottoman citizens send a petition to the local Ottoman consul in Iran, who was instructed to refer such cases to the religious officials of the same sect in the nearest Ottoman center where a ruling would then be made.[19]

Ottoman acceptance of Iran's capitulatory status resulted in increased government interest in the personal status of Ottoman and Iranian citizens. Government officials were concerned, apparently justifiably so, that Ottoman subjects would "fake" Iranian citizenship in order to escape from obligations to the Ottoman state. Similar abuses, as described above, had occurred with European subjects, particularly abuse of citizenship rights with regard to marriage (Masters 1991, 14).

Procedures and Punishments

Article 2 of the 1874 prohibition stated explicitly, "Those [officials] who are authorized to perform marriages and who act against the prohibition, will be held responsible." Religious officials such as imams and civil servants such as *muhtars* (elders of village or city quarters) were the officials concerned with personal status matters such as marriages. In 1887, the Meclis-i Vükela confirmed, "imams and *muhtars* who are authorized to perform marriages, who act against the prohibition, will be punished."[20] This reaffirmation of the responsibilities of imams and *muhtars* was in line with Tanzimat centralizing reforms and, particularly, the 1881 Law of Population Registration *(Sicill-i Nüfus Nizamnamesi),* which was the first regulation of census and population collection. This law required registration of marriages within six months of the contract. At the time the registration law was enacted, there was no centralized authority to record

19. BOA, HR.HMŞ.İŞO 7–1/3, 6 Mayıs 1326 (19 May 1910) and 12 Temmuz 1326 (25 June 1910). Also HR.HMŞ.İŞO 7–1/1, various dates including 13 Nisan 1326 (26 Aprıl 1909); 2 Mayıs 1326 (15 May 1910); and 6 Mayıs 1326 (19 May 1910).

20. BOA, M.V. 30–16, 2 Rebiyülahir 1305 (18 December 1887).

personal statistics. Although lack of registration did not affect the legality of the marriages, enforcement of the law remained ineffective until a new law of 1902 put into place penalties for officials who did not register marriages and other vital statistics such as birth and deaths (Duben and Behar 1991, 15–21, 108–9; Behar 2004, 540).

Cases of Ottoman officials who performed marriages despite the prohibition periodically came to the attention of government officials. In 1906, an official memorandum reached the Cabinet from Konya Province concerning an imam, Hacı Hafez Mahmed Efendi, who had solemnized a marriage between Fatma bint-i İsmail, an Ottoman citizen, and Habib bin Fettah, an Iranian. The memorandum asked for the correct punishment.[21] The Cabinet decided that the proper course of action was to exile the imam to another locality *(mahal).* In 1920, the Interior Ministry increased the penalty by compelling exile outside the borders of the Ottoman state for officials who performed marriages between Ottoman women and Iranian men.[22]

Imams who were Iranian citizens were also subject to the same punishments as Ottoman religious officials. No time was wasted in carrying out the punishment of exile for Ali Efendi, an imam apparently loosely affiliated with the Iranian Embassy, who was accused of performing a marriage between Arif bin Hacı Ali, an Iranian citizen from Tahtakale, and Mudanyalı Sabire Hanım, an Ottoman citizen. Imam Ali Efendi was not an official of the Embassy and therefore could not benefit from extraterritorial privileges and was liable for punishment.[23]

Punishments for couples who married despite the prohibition were outlined in March of 1888 when the Cabinet issued the following explanation of procedures to the provinces:

21. BOA, M.V. 113–139, 12 Cemaziyülevvel 1324 (4 July 1906).

22. BOA, Dahiliye Nezareti İdare-i Umumiye (DH.İUM) 19–23/5–75, 15 Mart 1336 (15 March 1920).

23. BOA, DH.İUM 19–23/5–71, 2 Haziran 1331 (15 June 1915); also HR.HMŞ. İŞO 7–1/2, 26 Kanunusani 1332 (8 February 1917); DH.İUM 19–23/5–73, 27 Safer 1336 (12 December 1917).

> Those who marry against the prohibition will be exiled. . . . [T]he majority of those claiming Iranian citizenship are found in Baghdad . . . and instructions [are forwarded] to Baghdad and to the provinces for the registration of these sort of persons so that Ottoman citizens are not inclined to enter Iranian citizenship. Carrying out of the aforesaid precautionary measures and procedures is sufficient for the prevention of these marriages in the Ottoman State.
>
> This decision concerns Iranians whose true nationality is not in doubt. The same decision is given to those who settled permanently in Ottoman territory and entered under the local laws of Ottoman citizenship. These kinds of persons will be expelled from Ottoman territories.
>
> . . . [I]t is not possible to prevent the wives of Iranians from willingly accompanying their husbands into exile.[24]

In later rulings, however, exile for the wives became the preferred form of punishment. In the 1906 official memorandum mentioned above, concerning punishments for Fatma bint-i İsmail, the Ottoman citizen, and Habib bin Fettah, her Iranian husband, officials considered whether in such cases the wives of Iranians, as well as their husbands, should be expelled within fifteen days. The Cabinet determined that Fatma would be exiled along with her husband, and this ruling should apply to all similar cases.[25]

In 1914, the Ministry of the Interior was informed about the case of Darıcalı Behice, an Ottoman citizen, who had married Ahmed Ağa, an Iranian living in Tuzla. The wedding ceremony was allegedly performed in the Iranian Embassy by an Iranian *hoca,* Seyyid Efendi, who lived behind the Valide Han mosque, the center of Iranian commerce in Istanbul. The Iranian Embassy claimed to have no knowledge of the performance of the ceremony; was sorry for the implications of the event; and requested punishment for those involved. The Interior Ministry determined that

24. BOA, HR.HMŞ.İŞO 7–1/1, 6 Receb 1305 (19 March 1888); also M.V. 30–16, 2 Rebiyülahir 1305 (18 December 1887); Y.MTV 34–39, 11 Zilkade 1305 (20 July 1888).

25. BOA, M.V. 113–139, 12 Cemaziyülevvel 1324 (4 July 1906).

both Ahmed and Behice, having married despite the prohibition, should be expelled immediately from the Ottoman State.[26]

In 1915, the Ministry of the Interior asked the legal advisors to the Office of the Grand Vizier whether banishment was to remain the punishment for couples who married against the prohibition. The advisors emphasized that every state had the right to expel foreigners and cited a decree dated 15 March 1915 clearly establishing that Iranians who married Ottoman women against the prohibition would be expelled. As a further clarification, the advisors cited the Second Supplement of Article 200 of the Criminal Law, which outlined a punishment of imprisonment of one to six months for husbands who married without obtaining marriage licenses and punishment of two months to one year for those who performed marriages without a license, because "a marriage license from the court is necessary."[27] Since the only way for Iranians to marry thus would be without a license, the advisors found that they must first of all be punished by imprisonment and then expelled from the Ottoman State.

From as early as the sixteenth century until the end of the empire, judges *(kadıs)* had the duty to rule on the legality of marriage contracts. A couple had to obtain a marriage license *(izinname)* from the judge, who would certify that there were no legal impediments to their marriage. The imam who performed the marriage ceremony was legally required to ask for this license, but more often than not, marriages were performed without a license from the judge. If the imam knew at least one of the parties to the marriage, he might overlook lack of a license (Duben and Behar 1991, 110–12). As late as 1920, in an effort to insure the continuation of the prohibition of marriages with Iranians, the Interior Ministry reaffirmed that marriage contracts between Muslims could only be performed by imams

26. BOA, DH.İUM 30–2/1, various dates from 25 Cemaziyülevvel 1332 (21 April 1914) to 20 Temmuz 1330 (2 August 1914); also DH.İUM 19–23/5–70, 23 Cemaziyülevvel 1333 (8 April 1915); DH.İUM 19–23/5–72, 22 Haziran 1331 (5 July 1915).

27. BOA, HR.HMŞ.İŞO 7–1/1, 26 Kanunusanı 1332 (8 February 1917); also see DH.İUM 19–23/5–74, 19 Şevvel 1335 (8 August 1917).

upon receipt of permits that were issued by the Shari'a courts. These permits were to be issued after inspection of the spouses' identity papers, that were obtained from the elders of the community.[28]

In 1920, the Cabinet considered the case of a deceased Iranian named Hacı 'Abbas Efendi bin Müteveffa. The late Hacı 'Abbas Efendi had lived in the neighborhood of Topkapı, and his wife, Münevver Hanım bint-i Hacı Mehdi, was an Ottoman citizen. The marriage had occurred thirteen years earlier and there were two children, one nine and the other six years of age at the time of the case. No eyewitnesses to the marriage could be found, and the imam who had performed the marriage had since died. At issue was whether, under such circumstances, the wife and children should be sent into exile. The Cabinet took a more conciliatory tone with regard to the exiling of the wives and children of deceased Iranian citizens. They decided that many years had passed since the marriage was concluded, and as there were no known witnesses, exiling the family members would force them into poverty and would "not be suitable to the right course of justice."[29] In such circumstances, it was reasonable to consider that the government may have ruled against punishment in favor of upholding other important responsibilities of citizenship such as payment of taxes and the requirement for army service.

The Ottomans reframed the concept of "dependent citizenship" of married women, the basis of the Law of Ottoman Nationality, by enacting the one exception to that law that reflected the special geopolitical exigencies in their political arena at the end of the nineteenth century—the necessity of maintaining control over the provinces of Iraq. Although the Ottoman need to control the Iraqi provinces would eventually be overshadowed by war and the devolution of the provinces, the 1874 prohibition of marriages between Ottoman women and Iranian men was, nevertheless, continually reaffirmed during the remaining half-century of

28. BOA, DH.İUM 19–23/5–77, 15 Ağustos 1336 (15 August 1920); also DH.İUM 19–23/5–78, 16 Eylül 1336 (16 September 1920).

29. BOA, DH.İUM 19–23/5–76, 6 Nisan 1336 (6 April 1920); and M.V. 219–129, 20 Şevval 1338 (7 July 1920).

Ottoman existence. Geopolitical realities and shifting Ottoman-Iranian relations that mandated the 1874 law created many new challenges and confusions for Ottoman officials in carrying out their duty to enforce this exception to the 1869 Law of Ottoman Nationality.

Confusion and Contradictions

When we examine discussions in the various ministries and in the Cabinet concerning the only exception to the dependent status of married women in the 1869 nationality law—the 1874 prohibition of marriage between Ottoman women and Iranian men—it becomes clear that the meaning of this exemption was sometimes questioned by officials themselves, and contested and opposed by those excluded from Ottoman citizenship. These confusions and contradictions would remain throughout the reign of Abdülhamid II, and there would be no further clarity under the regime of the Committee of Union and Progress (CUP).

Although the 1874 law was intended to put to rest, once and for all, the issue of marriage between Ottoman and Iranian citizens, it did not in fact prevent the many problems that were to arise during the enforcement of the law. During the remaining five decades of the Ottoman Empire, many questions arose among local officials and the government ministries as to exactly who was to be included under the prohibition and how it was to be enforced. Confusion no doubt existed as a result of the contradiction between the 1874 prohibition and the 1875 Ottoman-Persian Convention, which allowed Iranian citizens the same capitulatory rights as nationals of other states. In Article 9 of the 1875 Convention, the Ottomans had confirmed that the effects of the nationality law of 1869 would now apply to Persian nationals as well. The Convention essentially cancelled the 1874 law, since it included the right of Iranian men to marry Ottoman women (Aitchison 1909, xii, lxiv–lxv).

This conflict between the 1874 law and 1875 Convention was clearly elucidated in 1881 when officials in Trabzon asked the General Secretariat of the Census Bureau *(Sicill-i Nüfus İdare-i Umumiyesi Tahrirat Kalemi)* to clarify the broader question of the legality of marriage between Ottoman women and foreign citizens. The matter was considered in the Cabinet, and the following determination was made:

> A prohibition does not exist concerning the marriages of Ottoman women with citizens from states, other than Iran. Establishing such a prohibition would be contrary to public law and would also result in women who themselves are foreigners being prohibited from marrying Ottoman citizens. In any case, the loss that would result from the change of citizenship of [Ottoman] women who are married with foreigners would correspond to the profit that would result from foreign women entering Ottoman citizenship through marriage with Ottoman citizens.
>
> The prohibition concerning marriages between Ottoman women and Iranian citizens, in force heretofore and recently confirmed by the *irade-i seniye,* remains still valid, as it used to be.[30]

The Cabinet's decision did not end the confusion over this issue, which continued for local officials. In 1909 and 1910, questions were sent from Bolu Province asking for the proper procedure to determine the broader question of the citizenship of Ottoman women who were married to foreign Muslim citizens. In making its decision, the Census Bureau referred to Article 7 of the 1869 nationality law and determined that, with the exception of marriages with Iranians—which the judges of the Shari'a had prohibited—Ottoman women who married foreign Muslim citizens immediately acquired the citizenship of their husbands.[31]

In defining the prohibition on the basis of Ottoman and Iranian citizenship, the 1874 law had made no distinction with regard to religious affiliation. In January of 1890, the Cabinet received a request from Basra to clarify the status of Ottoman Christian women who married Iranians. The Cabinet referred to the provisions of the 1874 prohibition and responded that any woman who was an Ottoman citizen married to an Iranian citizen had done so against the prohibition. In the case of an Ottoman Christian woman, therefore, both the woman and her children

30. BOA, M.V. 62–42, 6 Receb 1308 (15 February 1891).

31. BOA, DH.MUİ 20–1/45, 15 Şaban 1327 (1 September 1909); Dahiliye Nezareti Sicill-i Nüfus İdare-i Umumiyesi Tahrirat Kalemi (DH. SN.THR) 3–9, 22 Rebiyülevvel 1328 (3 April 1910); also see DH.SN.THR 11–27, 7 Ağustos 1326 (20 August 1910).

were considered Ottomans and subject to the rights and responsibilities of citizenship.[32]

In 1892, however, the government added to provincial officials' confusion and contradicted itself over the question of the status of non-Muslim Ottoman citizens. The legal advisors to the Office of the Grand Vizier contradicted the Cabinet when they were asked to comment on the question of whether an Ottoman citizen who was Jewish was to be included in the prohibition. In this case, the advisors referred to the original law of 1822 and determined that there was no mention, of any kind, in that law regarding marriages of non-Muslim Ottoman citizens with Iranians. They also cited a decision of the Cabinet that held imams, in particular, responsible for solemnizing these marriages. As a result, the legal advisors determined that non-Muslim citizens were not included in the provisions of the law.[33] In 1895, a memorandum from the Foreign Ministry was sent to the Cabinet concerning Anton Efendi, the current Iranian Consul in Alexandretta, and a non-Muslim whose mother was an Ottoman citizen and whose father was the former Iranian Consul. The Cabinet was asked to determine whether, as a non-Muslim, he was libel to pay the tax imposed on non-Muslims in lieu of military service *(bedel-i askeri),* as his mother was an Ottoman citizen.[34] In this case the Cabinet referred to the theological basis of the 1874 law, declaring, "the goal of the prohibition was the prevention of the spread of Shi'ism in the Ottoman State, whose increase would result in conflicts between *mezheps.*" The Cabinet contradicted its earlier 1890 ruling and declared that the law did not extend to non-Muslims.[35]

In 1911, a request came from the Foreign Ministry to the Cabinet regarding a petition from Aydın Province asking for clarification of

32. BOA, M.V. 42–3, 13 Cemaziyülevvel 1307 (5 January 1890).

33. BOA, HR.HMŞ.İŞO 7–1/1, 15 Teşrinievvel 1308 (27 October 1892).

34. The *cizye* was converted into the *bedel-i askeri* in the *Islahat Fermanı* of 1856 during the Tanzimat in an attempt to eliminate the inequality of the poll tax that penalized non-Muslims. The solution was to establish the military exemption tax (see İnalcık 1973, 106).

35. BOA, M.V. 81–67, 26 Receb 1312 (23 January 1895).

whether the prohibition concerned not only Muslims but also non-Muslim Ottoman citizens who married Iranians. The Cabinet returned to its 1890 ruling and reiterated that Article 1 of the 1874 law, as in the past, in no way permitted these marriages because the purpose of the prohibition was to limit settlement by Iranians, which would otherwise multiply forever and anon *(mütemadiyen),* and, thereby, increase the number of foreigners in the Ottoman state. The prohibition, therefore, applied to all non-Muslim Ottoman citizens as well. By 1911, the Hamidian regime had been overthrown and the CUP was in power. The Cabinet's emphasis on nationality as a determining factor in its ruling may well reflect more of a recognition of a separate nation-state identity, and the importance of citizenship in this prohibition, whereas the Hamidian regime may have been more disposed to view the prohibition in light of the long-standing Shi'i-Sunni division.[36]

In August 1917, confusion regarding non-Muslim Ottoman-Iranian marriages was finally resolved when the Cabinet confirmed that the prohibition was for all Ottomans and Iranians, irrespective of religious affiliation. The Foreign Ministry had requested clarification from the Cabinet concerning the question of whether non-Muslim Ottoman women were included in the prohibition of marriages between Iranian men and Ottoman women. This time the Cabinet referred to Article 1 of the 1874 law, which prohibited marriages between Ottoman and Iranian citizens, and to Article 3, which stated that the women and children were considered Ottoman citizens and subject to conscription, military tax, and all other obligations of citizenship. The decision went on to state, "In view of the fact that conscription *(kur'a)* refers to Ottoman-Muslim citizens and military tax *(bedel-i askeri)* refers to non-Muslim Ottoman citizens, the law is intended for both Muslim and non-Muslim Ottoman citizens. Marriages with Iranian citizens, therefore, is prohibited for Muslim and non-Muslim Ottoman women."[37] The Interior Ministry issued a report in the

36. Hoover Institute Archives, Hiyadet Dağdeviren Collection (HIA-HDC) C I, no. 4, 30 Teşrin-i Sani 1327 (15 August 1911).

37. BOA, M.V. 209–24, 28 Şevvel 1335 (17 August 1917).

same month in response to a petition by an Iranian, Doctor Artinyan, requesting clarification of the legality of marriages between non-Muslim Ottoman women and non-Muslim Iranian men. The report upheld the prohibition on the same basis as cited by the Foreign Ministry.[38] Future discussions in the Cabinet would elevate the role of citizenship over religious difference as the primary motivation for the continuation of the marriage prohibition for Muslims and non-Muslims alike.[39]

Although the matter of non-Muslim Ottoman-Iranian marriages may have finally been resolved, questions also arose about the legality of marriages between Ottoman women and Sunni-Iranians. In 1892, the legal advisors to the Office of the Grand Vizier were asked to decide whether the marriage prohibition concerned only Shi'i Iranians or whether it included Sunni Iranian citizens as well. Without citing legal justifications, the legal advisors determined that marriages between Ottoman citizens and Sunni Iranians were also prohibited.[40]

The Ministry of the Interior received a telegraph from Baghdad in 1915 requesting clarification as to whether the prohibition of marriages concerned only Iranians and did not extend to the other Muslim peoples. An official memorandum by the Council of the Investigation of Religious Law *(Meclis-i tedkikat-i şer'iye)* stated:

> Marriage between the divisions of Islam is lawful. An adult Sunni male's marriage to a Mu'tezile or Shi'i [woman] is therefore lawful. But Sunni marriages to those who are in sects that curse [the Caliphs] and are followers of falsehoods—like [marriages] that have been repudiated or [are] within the prohibited degrees, are not lawful, even if [those who] deny the Almighty Creator, or the prophetic mission or the requirements of religion, or [those who follow] polytheism, claim to be from the sects [of Islam].[41]

38. BOA, Dahiliye Nezareti Mebani-i Emiriye ve Hapishaneler Müdüriyeti İdare Kalemi (DH.MB.HPS.M) 30/48, 10 Zilkade 1335 (28 August 1917).

39. BOA, M.V. 221–268, 24 Zilhicce 1339 (29 August 1921).

40. BOA, HR.HMŞ.İŞO 7–1/4, 8 Teşrinisani 1308 (20 November 1892).

41. BOA, DH.İUM E/7–60, 15 Cemaziyülevvel 1333 (31 March 1915).

The Council cited a *fetva* from the Chief Secretary of the Fetva Department *(Fetvahane Daire-i Meşihat-ı İslamiye Mektubi Kalemi),* which confirmed that the prohibition of marriage of Ottoman women with Iranians would benefit and advance the religion of the state. Citing Article 3 of the 1874 prohibition, the *fetva* confirmed that the law applied only to Iranians because "unfriendly relations remain at this time," and that it did not apply to other peoples of Islam.[42] Except for the singular prohibition against Algerians, discussed earlier, no prohibition has come to light against other Muslim peoples.

It should be pointed out that none of these rulings had any effect on Ottoman men who wanted to marry foreigners, even Iranian women. In 1892, the legal advisors to the Office of the Grand Vizier determined that marriages between Iranian women and Ottoman men were not included in the prohibition. This fact was reaffirmed in a case in 1911 sent from Bitlis province to the Ministry of the Interior regarding the proper registration of the citizenship of an Iranian woman who had married an Ottoman citizen. In this case the Census Bureau determined that "Ottoman citizens are not forbidden marriage to foreign women. These [marriages] are legal and the wife will acquire [the husband's] citizenship.[43]

Ottoman-Iranian geopolitical realities, particularly the empire's conflicts with Iran over their mutual frontier, were certainly evident in the discussions of the Ottoman legal advisers with respect to Ottoman-Iranian marriages. While the Shi'i-Sunni division remained the basis for the original prohibition and was an important part of the discussions in the various ministries and in the Cabinet, by the end of the Hamidian period, their deliberations were firmly rooted within the discourse of nationality and nationhood. If these marriages were legalized, then Ottoman women were required under the 1869 nationality law to take the citizenship of their Iranian husbands. These women and their children would become

42. Ibid.

43. BOA, HR.HMŞ.İŞO 7–1/4, 8 Teşrinisani 1308 (20 November 1892); and DH.SN.THR 22–19, 5 Mayıs 1326 (18 May 1910) and 1 Cemaziyülevvel 1329 (30 April 1911).

Iranian citizens living in Ottoman territory. Of concern to the Ottoman administration was the potential for large-scale conversion of these wives to Shi'ism. Their children would automatically become members of their fathers' sect and be considered Shi'a as well. The various discussions in the Cabinet generated by requests from the provinces reveals the lack of clarity in the 1874 law, and difficulties with its enforcement. While continual requests for clarity from the provincial officials to the center was a common feature of Ottoman bureaucratic practice, the numerous requests for clarification over who was to be included in the prohibition may also suggest that the law and its enforcement mechanisms were not effective in preventing these marriages. At a fundamental level, the Ottomans were unable to penetrate into the very private realm of the domestic sphere and effect change that would support the state in its contest with Iran over its three border provinces.

4

The Impact of the Marriage Prohibition on the Rights and Responsibilities of Citizens

INHERENT IN THE CONCEPT OF CITIZENSHIP as constructed by the centralizing monarchies of the nineteenth century was the notion that the citizen was a member of a community, which was concerned with the collective interests of the state. The citizen had certain compulsory obligations to the state such as paying taxes and performing military service. In performing these duties, the citizen acquiesced to the political and social order imposed by the state. As the citizen was a member of a community, his loyalty to the state would result in economic welfare and political and social stability for both the individual and the community. Deviation from this loyalty had to be resisted because it could cause the community to fail.[1] When the Ottomans constructed their prohibition of marriages between Ottoman women and Iranian men in 1874, they had two primary concerns. The first was a fear that children born of these marriages who were conscripted into the army might have lost their loyalty to the empire and, in consequence, make unreliable members of the armed services. The second concern was that large tracts of land in the eastern provinces might be transferred into the hands of heirs who claimed Iranian citizenship.

1. See the introduction to this book for a discussion of the standard theorists of citizenship in the twentieth century, including Marshall 1950 and 1965; Mann 1987, 339–54; and Turner 1990, 189–217, and 2000, 28–48; Tilly 1995a, 1–17, and 1995b, 223–36. See also Janowitz 1980, 1–24; and van Gunsteren 1994, 47.

Obligation for Military Service, the Loyalty of the Army

Universal military conscription is one of the main institutions necessary to create a national army, and national armed forces are an institution essential to success in nation-building. Conscription is also often an essential obligation of citizens, who are called upon to defend the state.[2] Military conscription in the nineteenth and twentieth centuries has recently received attention from historians working on the economic impact of conscription in relation to wage and nonwage labor.[3] An examination of conscription as a social construction is just beginning. This chapter is one of the first studies of the obligation for military service within the broader discussion of Ottoman centralizing policies, and one of the first to recognize the importance of the demographics of the family for control of the obligation for military service.

The creation of a standing army through universal conscription was introduced during the American and French revolutionary periods. In August of 1793, the French decreed that every citizen had an obligation to serve in the military. The French system placed a great economic burden on young men and their families because it removed them from the labor market for eight or more years. The Prussian Law on Conscription of September, 1814, improved upon the French system by creating a tiered service, beginning with one to three years on the front lines, followed by a period in the reserves *(Landwehr),* and, lastly, service in the *Landstrum* militia, which was called upon only in the face of enemy attack (Lucassen and Zürcher 1999, 7–10).[4]

The Ottoman Empire was not far behind European states in recognizing the importance of universal conscription. Sultan Mahmud II (1808–1839) saw the need for a more professional army after being defeated by Mehmed 'Ali's conscripts in Syria in the war of 1831 to 1833. The Council of the Ministry of War *(Dar-ı Şura-yı Askeri),* established

2. See Janowitz 1980, 6; Fahmy 1999, 59–77; Helman 2000, 316–77.

3. See Lucassen and Zürcher 1999, 1–19.

4. The idea of the citizen-soldier began in ancient Greece and Rome, but premodern armies were composed of militia organized in towns and in the countryside.

in 1837, proposed a period of service of five years. The Noble Rescript of the Rose Garden *(Hatt-ı Şerif-i Gülhane)* of 1839 noted the need for more equitable distribution of military service among subjects throughout the provinces. The edict stated:

> Although, as we have said, the defense of the country is an important matter, and that it is the duty of all the inhabitants to furnish soldiers for that object, it has become necessary to establish laws to regulate the contingent to be furnished by each locality according to the necessity of the time, and to reduce the term of military service to four or five years. For it is at the same time doing an injustice and giving a mortal blow to agriculture and to industry to take, without consideration to the respective population of the localities, in the one more, in the other less, men than they can furnish; it is also reducing the soldiers to despair and contributing to the depopulation of the country by keeping them all their lives in the service. In short, without the several laws, the necessity for which has just been described, there can be neither strength, nor riches, nor happiness, nor tranquillity for the empire; it must, on the contrary, look for them in the existence of these new laws. (Zürcher 1999, 81)[5]

After universal military service was introduced in 1844, the Ottomans created the *Nizamiye* army, which used the Prussian model of conscription. Initially, conscripts *(muvazzaf)* served for five years, but this term was later reduced to four, three, and finally two years. After service, conscripts and those who were not recruited initially through the lottery served as reservists *(redifler)* for seven years. Detailed regulations for conscription were drawn up in the Regulation for Military Conscription *(Kur`a Nizamnamesi)* of 1848, which remained the model until new regulations were established in August, 1869. The 1869 regulations established a three-tiered system. Soldiers in the regular army *(Nizamiye)* served for four years. Reservists *(redifler)* served for an additional six years, but could be exempted if they were the sole breadwinners for their families, were over thirty-two years of age, or had not had their names drawn in the lottery.

5. This translation was taken from Hurewitz 1975, 114–15.

Finally, guards *(müstahfiz)* served for eight years; they were not expected to fight but were called upon to carry out law-and-order duties when the regular and reserve armies were in the field. A new *Kur'a Nizamnamesi*, enacted in 1871, codified these regulations, and in 1879, comprehensive clarifications were enacted that detailed the process of conscription, the requirements for exemptions, punishments for draft dodgers or others trying to avoid the draft, and rules for volunteers. Years of service were reduced from ten years to six years for regular soldiers, three years in active service, and three years in the active reserve. Finally, in 1909, the CUP reduced the years of service from three to two years for soldiers serving in unhealthy climates, particularly for the Sixth Army in Iraq and the Seventh Army in Yemen (Zürcher 1999, 81–84).

In the early stages of creating a national army, conscription was not evenly applied throughout the provinces, and it was still confined to Muslim males. Universal conscription would depend on a comprehensive and accurate census that could register all eligible males. The Ottomans began registering male heads of households in a census that took place from 1831 to 1838, and in another census in 1844 that was conducted especially for the purpose of conscription. Lack of census-takers, as well as local resistance to the draft among the population at large and particularly among the tribes, led to an undercounting of the population. Military service was generally unpopular because of the uncertain length of service, and because of the empire's inability to adequately feed, clothe, and equip its soldiers. Many soldiers died from starvation; from diseases such as cholera, typhus, and dysentery; or from their wounds. The unpopularity of military service led many soldiers to desert and led potential recruits to flee into the mountains or hide among the urban populations. Others would bribe officials or maim themselves in order to be kept out of, or to be released from, service. Penalties were harsh and inflicted not only on the soldiers themselves but also on local notables or family members who had to guarantee their service (Zürcher 1999, 84–86).[6]

6. See also Fahmy 1999, 59–77; Douwes 1999, 111–27; Moreau 1999, 129–37; Bein 2006, 285–86. In order to stop draft dodging, the Ottoman government required

Exemptions from service were also serious obstacles to the creation of a universal army. Groups permanently exempted included Istanbul-born residents (this was a long-standing exemption) as well as non-Muslims, residents of Mecca and Medina, members of the *ulema* and their *medrese* students, as well as high-ranking civil servants, judges, and Islamic jurisconsuls *(müftis)*. Other professionals, such as lower-ranking civil servants, policemen, and railway clerks, were called to serve only in case of national mobilization. An individual could also petition for exemption if he was the sole financial supporter of his family *(muinsiz)*. The first conscription law of 1848 established the *bedel-i şahsi*, a payment that allowed a recruit to personally buy his way out of serving by paying for someone to take his place. By the 1870s, a conscript no longer needed to find a replacement but could pay cash in lieu of service *(bedel-i nakdi)*. The cost was 5,000 kuruş, or 50 gold liras.

The Reform Rescript *(Islahat Fermanı)* of 1856, which emphasized equality for all subjects of the empire, was written to end discrimination between Muslims and non-Muslims. As equal citizens, non-Muslims should have been included in the draft lotteries. Non-Muslims, however, were not eager to be conscripted and generally preferred to pay the head tax *(cizye)* in lieu of military service. The government was also not interested in giving up the extensive revenues brought into the treasury by the head tax. Both the government and the army were also unwilling to arm non-Muslims, and not eager to include Jews and Christians, who, officials felt, could potentially dilute the religious fighting spirit of Ottoman forces. The Christians and Jews who did serve in the army were confined primarily to the medical officer corps. For these reasons, non-Muslims were not universally included in the draft until July of 1909, when military service became compulsory for all Ottomans. In October of 1909, under the CUP administration, Jews and Christians were finally taken

---

six annual conscription examinations for those of eligible age (between twenty to twenty-five years of age), and certification by military and civil officials. The examinations were, however, not difficult enough to prevent a certain degree of cheating by those attempting to avoid military service.

into service. They were still not armed, but instead were consigned to labor and repair work, and resupply services (Lucassen and Zürcher 1999, 11; Zürcher 1999, 88–90).[7]

Loyalty of the army was a concern common among all armies during the nineteenth and early twentieth centuries.[8] In the Ottoman Empire, the loyalty of the Sixth Army in Iraq was questionable because of the many decades of Shiʿi missionary activity in the provinces. Some reports suggested that as much as ninety percent of the Sixth Army was suspected of being Shiʿa (Çetinsaya 2006, 101–2). By 1885, the Cabinet turned its attention once again to marriages between Ottoman women and Iranian men, upholding Article 3 of the 1874 law prohibiting Ottoman-Iranian marriages and reaffirming that all male offspring were considered Ottoman citizens and liable for military service, no matter how many generations their families had lived in Ottoman territory.[9] This issue became a major bone of contention between the Ottoman and Iranian governments. Shortly after the 1885 decree, the Iranian government began a series of protests to the Cabinet, challenging the obligation for military service of the sons born of Ottoman women who were married to Iranian citizens.[10] They asked that children born before the publication of the 1874 law be exempted from military service, and that the Ottoman government not expel Iranians who married despite the prohibition. In response to the Iranian protest, the Cabinet reaffirmed the prohibition of these marriages. Ottoman officials expressed concern that if Ottoman women were permitted to marry Iranians they would do so in order to exempt their children from conscription. But they did allow an exemption from military service for children born before 1874. The Cabinet, furthermore, charged imams and court officials with the responsibility for

7. For a detailed examination of the exemption based on need and "sole financial support," see van Os 1999, 95–110.

8. One has only to look to the May 1917 mutiny of the French army to understand that their reliability on the battlefield was never certain (see Lucassen and Zürcher 1999, 10).

9. BOA, İrade Meclis-i Mahsus 3992, 19 Rebiyülevvel 1303 (26 December 1885).

10. BOA, M.V. 1–19, 18 Rebiyülahir 1302 (4 February 1885).

making certain that these marriages did not take place, and also for certifying which children were allowed the exemption. These decisions were communicated to Baghdad, Basra, Erzurum, Van, and Mosul, and to the field marshals of the Fourth and Sixth Armies. The communiqué also outlined ways to prevent Ottoman citizens from assuming Iranian citizenship. Iranians who married despite the prohibition were to be expelled immediately from the state. Children eligible for conscription, but who went abroad, were still required to perform their military service upon their return. The government repeated its apprehension over the spread of Shiʿism in the border region and called for registration of all persons claiming Iranian citizenship, especially in Baghdad and the villages where most Iranians resided.[11]

Resistance to recruitment could be more than just an individual decision. Such a decision affected the whole family and was often part of a "household strategy" that depended on several factors, including the advantage or disadvantage of military service for the family unit. Conscription could, for example, entail job opportunities and increased status or, conversely, risks and dangers that were deemed unacceptable. In the empire in general, and in Iraqi provinces in particular, the Ottomans needed certain institutions in order to effectively carry out a conscription system. They included a comprehensive census and registration, and the ability to gather and train troops. In Iraq, avoidance was made easier in the absence of such institutional requirements. Potential recruits could simply leave Ottoman lands or, as in the case of many Ottoman Greeks, Armenians, and Jews after 1909, change their nationality. Soldiers could also simply desert their ranks and cross borders (Lucassen and Zürcher 1999, 12–13).

The expansion of the armed forces became imperative for the Ottoman Empire after their defeat in the Ottoman-Russian War of 1877 to 1878. The government embarked on a series of reforms that included the Recruitment Regulation *(Ahz-ı Asker Nizamnamesi)* (AAN) enacted on

11. BOA, Y.A. HUS 212–24, 13 Rebiyülevvel 1303 (20 December 1885).

25 October 1886.[12] Article 32 required military service for the sons born of marriages between Ottoman women and Iranians. The article stated:

> With the exemption of Iranian citizens, citizens [and the children of citizens] from foreign countries who permanently reside, are married or move to a location [where they are] under the obligation of [a foreign] military, are exempt from military service.[13]

In November 1886, one month after the enactment of the AAN, the Iranian government demanded the repeal of both the 1874 law prohibiting these marriages and Article 32 of the AAN. The Iranians threatened retaliation: children born of Iranian women and Ottoman men would also be obligated to serve in the Iranian army.[14] This threat may have been an empty one since, although the Iranian government had attempted reforms similar to the Ottoman Tanzimat program, they had had little success in modernizing their army. Their reforms met with domestic obstacles from entrenched interests such as the *ulema,* local notables, and tribal chiefs who maintained their own military forces in the countryside, as well as the peasantry themselves, who were the primary target for recruitment. European powers, including Britain and Russia, also did not want to see these reforms succeed. Russia preferred to keep Iran weakened so it could not be a strong buffer for Britain. Britain, on the other hand, did not want to provoke a conflict with Russia over the Iranian reform program. The Iranians failed to create a standing army and did not succeed in establishing modern recruiting practices, officer training, or arms production. Their army consisted of the regular *nizami* infantry and artillery, which remained an ineffective force that drained the economy until they were finally disbanded in 1921. The irregular cavalry was not furnished by a

12. These regulations were part of a comprehensive program (discussed earlier) to reform the previous recruitment regulations. Sultan Abdülhamid II hoped that these efforts would expand "the recruitment base and establish a citizen army" (see Bein 2006, 288–94).

13. *Dustür,* 1. tertip, 5. cilt, s. 664.

14. BOA, M.V. 14–16, 16 Safer 1304 (14 November 1886).

conscription system, but was staffed from levies put on tribal chiefs. These soldiers remained in the service of their chiefs in their own districts, unless the government called them up for specific operations. Recruitment was not universal, but was based on an outdated system known as the *bunichah,* carried out through revenue assessments on the villages. Recruitment was suppose to apply to the whole country, but in reality it concentrated on the provinces that supplied the best soldiers. The actual numbers of soldiers under arms was unknown because of inaccurate record-keeping and corruption, which allowed salary payments to nonexistent soldiers. By the end of the nineteenth century, the Iranian military was in decline, and recruitment problems would not improve until universal conscription was created in the early twentieth century (Cronin 1997, 2–8).[15]

The Iranian threat to conscript children born of the marriages between Iranian women and Ottoman men was fundamentally an impotent, ineffective attempt to influence Ottoman policy. The Ottoman government denied the Iranian request for cancellation of the marriage prohibition and the requirement for military service.[16] In response, the Iranian Embassy continued its protests and

> strongly demanded its [Article 32 of the AAN] repeal . . . since the meaning of this article goes beyond the bounds of the sacred law of the Ottoman state. No state has the authority to carry out tyrannical procedures that are, in any case, unlawful. Let there not be interference with the wives and Iranian children of *şer'i* marriages, even if the prohibition of marriages between Ottoman women and Iranian citizens is deemed to be the requirement of the internal affairs of the Ottoman state. The articles will be considered [by the Iranian government] as nonexistent since they are contrary to the public laws of the

15. I chose not to discuss the Cossack Brigade and the Government Gendarmerie, both of whom were financed by Russia and Britain and were largely voluntary forces. Neither force was a part of the conscription process.

16. BOA, Y.A. RES 37–8, 12 Cemaziyülevvel 1304 (6 February 1887).

> state, which are clear and confirm that the wife and children follow the father.[17]

In this memorandum and in future communications, the Iranian government continually noted that the 1874 prohibition was in conflict with the "public laws of the [Ottoman] state," and demanded that Iranians receive the same rights as other foreigners under the 1869 Law of Ottoman Nationality. The Iranian ambassadors argued that the 1874 law was not enforceable because similar cases concerning other foreigners who had lived in Ottoman territories were not included in such a prohibition.[18] They continued to call for its cancellation and for the cancellation of Article 32 of the AAN. Although the Iranian government would eventually acquiesce to the Ottomans over the explusion of Iranian men who marry Ottoman women, it would continued to protest against Article 32, stating that the law could not be retroactive and that the children born before the law's publication should be exempt from conscription.[19]

In 1887, in response to continuing Iranian protests, the Cabinet met and reaffirmed the dangers of these marriages in the border provinces of Iraq:

> the matter of these marriages with Iranians, which as time passes multiply in Ottoman territories and especially in the vicinity of the Iranian borders, creates a grievous calamity [and] for this reason it becomes necessary to strongly prevent these marriages, [as they] cause bad consequences in all of the provinces of the Empire and mostly in the Iraqi

17. BOA, İrade Meclis-i Mahsus 4111, 10 Cemaziyülahir 1304 (6 March 1887).

18. BOA, İrade Meclis-i Mahsus 4111, 10 Cemaziyülahir 1304 (6 March 1887); M.V. 27–32, 13 Rebiyülahir 1305 (29 December 1887); M.V. 27–49, 24 Rebiyülahir 1305 (9 January 1888).

19. BOA, M.V. 17–49, 3 Cemaziyülahir 1304 (27 February 1887); M.V. 15–18, 25 Receb 1304 (19 April 1887); M.V. 30–16, 2 Rebiyülahir 1305 (18 December 1887); Sadaret Mektubi Kalemi Mühimme Kalemi Odası (A. MKT.MHM) 499–16, 3 Receb 1306 (5 March 1889) and 26 Şevval 1306 (25 June 1889).

> region among the tribes and [in] all the major cities like Baghdad, Karbala', Necef, Basra, and Mosul.[20]

In March 1888, the Cabinet again answered a protest from the Iranian Embassy, and reaffirmed that the obligation for military service of children born of these marriages was covered in the 1874 prohibition as well as by Article 32 of the AAN. An exemption from military service would only be given to male children born before the publication date of the AAN. All others would be obligated for military service upon reaching the age of conscription.[21] Partially in response to continuing Iranian protests, the Ottoman judiciary sent out a memorandum to provincial prosecutors on 25 October 1888 reiterating that these marriages were prohibited, and if they occurred, the Iranians involved should be exiled at once from the Ottoman state. The purpose of the law was to prevent Ottoman citizens from desiring to enter into Iranian citizenship. *Muhtars* and imams who performed marriages, and did not take care to protect the laws of the state, would be punished.[22]

Although the exact numbers of Iranian citizens in the Iraqi provinces were not known because of the difficulties discussed earlier in carrying out census counts in the region, periodic reports from provincial officials suggested that the numbers were substantial enough to warrant concern and immediate attention. A report from the Vali of Baghdad, Mustafa Asim, in January of 1888, described the situation in the province as follows:

> there are approximately fifteen thousand to twenty thousand residents of Baghdad province [some] who claim that they are by origin Iranians [and others] who have married and settled here one hundred years ago, fifty years, or more recently having migrated to Baghdad

20. BOA, İrade Meclis-i Mahsus 4111, 10 Cemaziyülahir 1304 (6 March 1887); M.V. 25–75, 20 Safer 1305 (7 November 1887).

21. HIA-HDC, C I, 2.

22. *Ceride-i Mehakim* (Journal of the Courts), 22 Teşrin-i evvel 1304 (3 November 1888), issue 469, page 5425. I wish to thank Avi Rubin for alerting me to this notification and its publication.

for numerous reasons, acquired local jurisdiction, and abandoned the Iranian language and customs.[23]

In March 1888, the Cabinet reaffirmed the obligation for military service:

> The children who result from these marriages, and who remain in Ottoman territories, will be held liable for military service upon reaching military age. As for those Iranians who were expelled as a result of the decision to marry against the prohibition, and who return after a short time . . . [they] will be obligated to perform military service upon reaching military age.[24]

Procedures were created to identify Ottoman citizens who were liable for conscription. The Commission of Military Inquiry *(Teftiş-i Askeri Komisyonu)* was established to investigate and propose a plan for registering the population.[25] In 1897, the Commission recommended that young men who reached military age should be registered on the fifteenth of November of each year and that those lists should then be turned over to local military officials. Youths who had not registered were to be seized and conscripted into the army. The Iranian consuls-general were asked for lists of Iranian citizens under their protection. When no names were provided, the Ottoman government advised the provinces that they should take it upon themselves to register this group. Each case was to be investigated individually, and no exemptions were to be given until it could be determined exactly when and why the Iranians had settled in the Iraqi provinces.[26]

In specific cases that reached the Cabinet during the remaining decades, they continually reaffirmed the obligation of military service.

23. BOA, İrade Meclis-i Mahsus 4111, 12 Cemaziyülevvel 1305 (26 January 1888).

24. BOA, HR.HMŞ.İŞO 7–1/1, 6 Receb 1305 (19 March 1888); Y.MTV 34–39, 11 Zilkade 1305 (20 July 1888); HIA-HDC, C I, no. 1, 10 Receb 1305 (23 March 1888).

25. BOA, İrade Meclıs-i Mahsus 4111, 12 Cemaziyülevvel 1305 (16 January 1888); M.V. 26–62, 19 Rebiyülevvel 1305 (5 December 1887); M.V. 27–70, 5 Cemaziyülevvel 1305 (19 January 1888); M.V. 28–31, 23 Cemaziyülevvel 1305 (6 February 1888).

26. BOA, Y.MTV. 169–38, 12 Cemaziyülahir 1315 (8 November 1897).

In 1892, for example, the legal advisers to the Office of the Grand Vizier were asked to decide whether non-Muslim children born of these marriages were required to pay the military tax *(bedel-i askeri).* At issue was the citizenship of three hundred to four hundred non-Muslim children of Iranian fathers who were married to Ottoman women and were living in Aleppo. The legal advisers cited Article 3 of the 1874 law that made children born of these marriages liable for conscription, military tax, and all other taxes of the state. As a result, the advisers determined that non-Muslim children of Iranian fathers were included in the payment of military tax.[27] In 1910, the Cabinet considered the request for exemption from military service of a man named Mehmed Hasan, an Iranian who had become an Ottoman citizen in 1880–1881. The Cabinet determined that "foreigners" who had settled in Ottoman territory and had taken Ottoman citizenship were required to perform military duty as long as they were not required to perform military service in their former country of citizenship.[28] In 1914, the Interior Ministry was confronted with a family of seventeen persons from Kirkuk who claimed to be Iranian citizens, allegedly for the purpose of avoiding military service. The father was from the Koylu tribe and had settled in Kirkuk some forty years earlier. The Ministry determined that since the children were registered in the census and at the time of registration they had not proven their claim to be Iranian citizens, they were considered eligible for immediate conscription.[29]

The Iranian government continued to protest and attempt to persuade the Ottoman government to cancel the 1874 marriage prohibition and Article 32 of the AAN. Even during the Constitutional Period, the legal advisors continued to reaffirm the prohibition of Ottoman-Iranian marriages, and the obligation for military service of the sons born from these marriages. Those who married despite the prohibition would be

27. BOA, HR.HMŞ.İŞO. 7–1/4, 13 Mayıs 1308 (25 May 1892).

28. BOA, DH.SN.THR 10–65, 27 Cemaziyülahir 1328 (6 July 1910).

29. BOA, Dahiliye Nezareti İdari Kısım Belgeleri (DH.İD) 30–2/53, 8 Safer 1332 (6 January 1914).

expelled and the male children who remained in the Ottoman state would be obliged for military service upon reaching the age of conscription. Children expelled with their parents, who later returned to the Ottoman state, would also be obligated for military service.[30] During the Constitutional Period, the army was confronted with a lack of manpower and, by necessity, searched for all available soldiers for defense of the empire (Deringil 1998, 69). In examining the specific case of Ottoman attempts to recruit a loyal population into the armed service, it is clear that universal conscription as a mechanism for nation-building, and as a means to secure the borders, met with failure, not only in the empire as a whole, but in the provinces of Iraq as well (Zürcher 1999, 79–94). The lack of adequate institutions for census-taking, the widespread availability of exemptions (particularly with the nomadic tribal populations), and the ability to pay the exemption tax *(bedel-i nakdi)* led to an army primarily composed of Anatolian peasants, not a universally conscripted army that was loyal to the imperial nation.

The Disposition of Estates and the Loss of Ottoman territory

Land Law and Private Property

The proliferation of land reform decrees and laws enacted during the nineteenth century (see the introduction) reflected a centralization process that sought to create prosperity and security of property, and created a bureaucratic system that would transform freehold *(mülk)* land into a single-titleholder-and-taxpayer system. The Ottomans established provincial and local councils and departments to enforce a more equitable system of registration and taxation, and a single property tax *(vergi resmi),* which linked the registration of taxable property to the individual—the individuation of tax responsibility.

The centralizing process was successful in some areas but not in others. The regulations of the 1840s, which established a single property tax

30. BOA, HR.HMŞ.İSO 7–1/1, 25 Cemaziyülahir 1327 (14 July 1909) and HR.HMŞ.İSO 7–1/1, 1 Kanunusani 1327 (14 January 1912).

and the registration of taxable property, were more successful in Anatolia and Rumeli than in the Arab provinces because of the lack of infrastructure in the latter to carry out the registration (İslamoğlu 2000, 10–11; Mundy and Smith 2007, 40–45). In tribal areas such as Kurdistan and the southern provinces of Iraq, the government favored policies to settle nomadic tribes over claims by the peasants to the land. Wealthier individuals could disenfranchise peasants by calling in debts to acquire peasant rights to titles. In settled areas, however, those peasants who did acquire the titles to their land or to uncultivated state land, could establish their ownership to private property. It is important to note that ownership was not an absolute right, but instead a right to production and land revenues (Salzmann 1999, 47; İslamoğlu 2000, 26).

In subsequent decades, administrative law regulated all aspects of land transactions in order to acquire the fullest amount possible of tax revenues. Provincial and property laws enacted in the 1860s and 1870s established local councils and provincial departments for the administration of property, registration, and taxation. Survey teams were sent out to ensure the registration of all land (İslamoğlu 2000, 26–31). As noted earlier, the Tanzimat Reforms were more successful wherever the Ottomans exercised direct rule. Imposing the reforms in areas where local interests still ruled—outside of provincial centers and in frontier regions—proved more difficult.

Property Ownership and Inheritance among Foreigners

In the 1860s, the Ottoman Empire enacted a series of laws that attempted to control the rights of non-Muslim Ottomans and foreigners to buy and transfer immovable property. In an 1866 law concerning the regulation of persons protected by foreign consulates *(Protégés des Consulats)*, the Ottomans confirmed capitulatory privileges to property ownership and transmissibility of such property upon death to Ottoman subjects under foreign protection and to the employees of foreign consulates (Young 1905, 2:234–35; Rafeq 2000, 177). Under pressure from foreign governments, the Ottomans expanded further the rights of foreigners in an imperial decree in 1867, which gave foreigners the right to own immovable property in the empire, with the exception of land in the Hijaz. This concession had been already agreed upon in the Reform Rescript of 1856, but before the 1867 decree, foreigners were only able to rent immovable property, or to own it in partnership with an Ottoman subject. The preamble to the 1867 decree detailed its specific purpose, which was:

> to secure the extension of wealth and prosperity in the Ottoman empire [*sic*], and to remove difficulties, abuses, and doubts of all kind that arise by reason of foreign subjects' becoming possessors of property *(emlak),* and to place this important matter under a firm law, and to complete financial and civil security. (Rafeq 2000, 181, 227)

While the right of foreigners to own land was being regularized in legislation, Fuad Paşa (the foreign minister) and Mehmed Emin 'Ali Paşa (the grand vizier) were attempting to negotiate an agreement that would require Europeans to forgo the protections of the capitulatory system and become liable to the same local laws, regulations, and taxation as Ottoman subjects. The 1867 decree, however, subverted this aim by stating that police or other Ottoman authorities could not enter the residences of foreign owners without the permission of their consuls. This, in effect, led to the unenforceability of any Ottoman laws pertaining to land in foreign ownership (Owen 1993, 119–20).[31] The protocol had to be accepted and signed by foreign governments in order for their nationals to receive the benefits of the decree.

The acquisition of land by Christian and non-Ottoman Muslim foreigners was a long-standing concern for the Ottoman government, and control over this process was an essential part of the Ottomans' policy of centralization over its peripheral provinces. Real estate and wealth acquisition by non-Ottoman Muslims from the British, French, Russian, and Dutch empires, in particular, was considered a threat to the security of the Iraqi provinces and to the empire as a whole (Deringil 2003, 329; 1998, 57). Inevitably, the purchase of real estate by foreigners became a

31. The protocol stated *"ne porte aucune atteinte aux immunitées consacrées par les traités et qui continueront à courier la personne et les biens meublés des étrangers devenus proprietaires d'immeubles."*

major issue when they died. A law of 5 March 1883 stated that Ottoman subjects who changed their nationality before or after the enactment of the Law of Ottoman Nationality of 1869 would enjoy the same rights as foreign subjects, if the nation under which they now owed allegiance had accepted the 1867 decree, which gave foreigners the right to own property, and had signed the protocol. The Ottoman government was, however, fundamentally unwilling to allow immovable property to fall into the hands of foreigners, so whenever possible they investigated and challenged the citizenship status of the deceased. One outstanding case was that of Muhammed Kasimbaev, who had migrated from Russian Central Asia in 1884 and had taken Ottoman citizenship at the time of his arrival. When he died in 1893, the Russian authorities maintained that he had not taken Ottoman citizenship because no passport could be found among his belongings. The Russian Foreign Ministry, therefore, considered him a Russian subject and requested that all of his belongings be returned to his relatives in Russia. The dispute continued for two years, with the Russians requesting the return of his personal effects and the Ottomans maintaining that he was an Ottoman subject and therefore the Russians had no claim (Meyer 2007, 24–25).

Marriages between Ottomans and foreigners, and the accumulation of Ottoman resources by foreigners as a result of those marriages, added a new dimension to the interests of the Ottoman government in controlling its territory. Inheritance matters were particularly relevant because the 1867 decree raised questions about the inheritance rights of Ottoman women who were married to foreign nationals and had acquired the nationality of their husbands. In such a case, if the woman died before her adopted country had signed the 1867 protocol, would her husband and children (who also took the nationality of their father) inherit her property in the empire? Under Article 110 of the Ottoman Land Code of 1858, children with foreign citizenship had been denied the right to inherit from a mother who given up her Ottoman citizenship. A memorandum *(tezkere)* of 21 June 1873 from the Office of the Grand Vizier to the Foreign Ministry stated that, under the circumstances outlined above, neither the foreign husband nor his children could inherit the wife's property (Rafeq 2000, 184–85).

The matter of the inheritance rights of Ottoman women who married Iranian men was of concern, particularly after the 1874 law prohibiting these marriages, which denied Ottoman women the opportunity to acquire the Iranian citizenship of their husbands. The disposition of estates of Iranian citizens who lived in Ottoman territory had long been a sensitive matter between the two states because it represented legal control of Ottoman territory by Iranian citizens. The two states had addressed the issue in treaties before the 1874 law, but violations of treaty provisions continued to occur, especially in the Iraqi provinces, where Ottoman governors were known to confiscate Iranian property.[32]

The issue of inheritance had specific resonance in the text of Mahmud II's 1822 mandate prohibiting marriage between Ottomans and Iranians. The wording of the mandate left no doubt that the matter of inheritance was being addressed in the law. Unlike earlier *fetvas*, the prohibition of 1822 was gender-specific, expressly prohibiting marriages between Ottoman-Sunni women and Iranians, Shi'ites, heretics, or "persons of unknown lineage." According to the mandate, it was imperative that children and grandchildren know their origins, and marrying persons of unknown lineage would deny them this right. In addition, if no prohibition of Ottoman-Iranian marriages existed, the children of such marriages would automatically be regarded as Shi'a. This matter was to acquire urgency later in the nineteenth century when, under the 1869 Law of Ottoman Nationality, both the wife and her children would assume Iranian citizenship. Their children would automatically take the religion of their father and be considered Shi'ites. If that was the case, not only would a change of allegiance seriously call into question the loyalty of Ottoman subjects to the state, but, as a practical matter, wealth from moveable and immovable property would be transferred out of Ottoman hands and into the coffers of Iranian citizens and possibly the Iranian state.

Following the 1822 mandate, the 1823 and 1848 Treaties of Erzurum were the next enactments to address the disposition of Iranians' estates. These treaties had an economic component that became increasingly

32. For a discussion of the treaties, see Masters 1991, 6–7.

important as the century progressed, and this became one of the primary motivations for restatements of the prohibition. The treaties extended the status of Iranians even further than previous agreements, and, for the first time, provided that reforms would be undertaken in the disposition of the estates of Iranians who died in the Ottoman Empire. The issue of abuse of Iranian pilgrims by local Ottoman authorities had been a contentious and continual problem for the two governments. Such matters included unfair taxation, the imposition of the head tax *(cizye)* on non-Muslim Iranians, and the confiscation of the estates of those who had died while living in, or passing through, Ottoman territory.[33] Iranian leaders had been pushing for reforms for more than a century, by the time of the Erzurum treaties. According to Islamic law, the estates of Muslims who died without heirs reverted to the state. Before the treaties, Ottoman officials often seized property outright, or they would hold property for only up to six months while awaiting claimants, after which it would revert to the state treasury. The Iranian government had long argued that six months was not enough time for heirs to be notified in Iran and travel to Ottoman territory to claim the estate. One outstanding example of this problem occurred in 1610, when two brothers from Hamadan in Iran died while on a caravan between Baghdad and Aleppo with 200,000 pieces of gold in their possession. Their estates were seized and quickly sent to Istanbul, apparently without any attempt to locate heirs (Masters 1991, 8).

In the eighteenth century, the Ottoman government issued two edicts that attempted to address this problem. In 1706, the Ottomans gave Iranians the right to handle the estates of their deceased without the interference of local Ottoman officials. More detailed regulations were enacted in 1724, when the Ottomans allowed the estates of deceased Iranians to be transferred directly to their heirs in the Ottoman Empire, or

33. This is by no means to suggest that the Ottoman government put into effect an official policy of abuse of Iranian pilgrims. Other Muslim pilgrims also complained of abusive behavior. These occurrences seemed to be of a local nature, undertaken by corrupt regional and local officials who were not under the control of the central administration (see Masters 1991, 6–7).

to be assigned to an officially designated companion of the deceased who was entrusted with the inventory of the estate, with determining whether heirs existed, and with carrying the estate back to heirs in Iran. If there were no heirs, then the estate became the property of the Ottoman treasury (Masters 1991, 8). These edicts were either not enforced or simply ignored on the local level. In the eighteenth century, for example, governors of Damascus were known to have confiscated the estates of Persians who died while on pilgrimage (Rafeq 1966, 60). In Baghdad province, when more than seven hundred Iranians died during the plague of 1773, Ömer Paşa al-Da'ud (1764–1775), the Mamluk governor who was better known for amassing power than for serving the Ottoman Empire, confiscated their estates to supplement his income without redress to their heirs. Although the shah complained about this injustice to Sultan Abdülhamid I, the sultan had little power over the distant province or its governor and could not address Iranian concerns (Perry 1987, 63; 1979, 171–72; Finkel 2005, 407).[34]

The Treaties of Erzurum attempted one final time to settle the matter of Persian subjects who did not have heirs present at the time of death. It stated:

> the Officers of the Treasury *(Beyt ül-Mal)* shall . . . register the property. . . . For a period of one year the effects shall be lodged . . . until the lawful heir or administrator of the estates may arrive, when, according to the Register of the Courts of Jurisdiction, the property shall be delivered up. (Hurewitz 1975, 221)

The issue of the estates of Iranians who died in Ottoman territory was just one example of the multitude of problems that confronted these two empires as the Ottomans tried to control their Iraqi provinces. The

34. It should be noted that the Ottomans were not the only monarchs to confiscate property of foreigners who died on their soil. One of the motivations for applying for naturalization in France in the eighteenth century was to inherit property. Under French law the king could confiscate the estates of foreigners who died without a naturalized or native heir (see Gordon 2003, 243).

transfer of immovable property through inheritance to Iranian citizens became a more urgent problem during the Tanzimat period, as laws were enacted that restricted government confiscation of property of Ottoman nationals, established the right to some measure of private ownership, and allowed foreigners the right to own land in the empire (Sousa 1933, 81–82; Ahmad 1984, 57; Owen 2000, xvi, xvii).[35] Marriages between Ottoman women and Iranian men complicated the problem and focused attention on the fact that immoveable property could come under Iranian ownership. In the Iraqi frontier provinces, this was an urgent matter because, if marriages between Ottoman women and Iranian men were allowed, wealth from moveable and immovable property could be transferred out of Ottoman hands into the estates of wives and children who were Iranian citizens. The issue of inheritance was one of the important reasons for the 1874 law, which created an exception to the 1869 Law of Ottoman Nationality by denying Ottoman women and their children the right to acquire Iranian citizenship.

Almost immediately upon publication of the 1874 law prohibiting Ottoman-Iranian marriages, the Ottoman government began to receive requests from various provinces for information about the disposition of the estates of Iranians. The government reaffirmed that, as in the past, the Iranian consuls would handle cases between Iranians. If an Ottoman citizen brought a case against the estate of an Iranian living in the Ottoman Empire, the case would be handled in local courts, like other legal cases. If the Iranian citizen had taken Ottoman citizenship, the case would be handled according to Ottoman law.[36] As might be expected, the Iranian government, through its embassy in Istanbul, launched a number of protests concerning the moveable possessions and immoveable property of deceased Iranians who had lived in the empire.[37]

35. Huri Islamoğlu argues that individual property rights allowed the central government to extend its reach directly into the countryside through the registration of land and levy of taxes by state agencies (see Islamoğlu 2000, 8).

36. BOA, Y.A. RES 7–2, 12 Muharrem 1291 (1 March 1874).

37. BOA, Y.A. RES 19–29, 1 Cemaziyülevvel 1299 (21 March 1882); Y.A. RES. 20–41, 5 Receb 1300 (12 May 1883).

In 1886, the problem of the inheritance shares of daughters born from these marriages was brought to the attention of the Cabinet. Cevahiri Mirza Hadi, an Iranian who had taken Ottoman citizenship twenty-six years earlier and who resided in Baghdad, had one son and two daughters. The director of the Baghdad registration office asked whether a one-half share was legal for the daughters. The Cabinet responded that the son of an Ottoman woman married to an Iranian, in every case, was considered an Ottoman citizen and had the legal right to succession. Regarding the daughters, in order to claim the right to succession, they were required to have changed their citizenship to that of their father. It was first necessary to determine whether the daughters were Ottoman or Iranian citizens, and if they had not become Ottoman citizens, they would be deprived of their shares. This is an unusual case, because in Ottoman archival documents and laws, no gender distinction was made as to whether daughters, as well as sons, were considered Ottoman citizens. Nowhere in the documents did Ottoman officials mention that only sons were considered Ottoman citizens. This directive clearly shows, however, that the male children born from these marriages were automatically considered Ottoman citizens, but the female children might take the citizenship of their fathers and be counted as Iranian citizens unless they chose to request Ottoman citizenship. In 1887, upon further requests for clarification as to whether the daughters should be deprived of their inheritance, the Cabinet reversed its opinion and decided that, on the basis of religious law, the property should be divided among the heirs according to the system of the Shari‘a, and that daughters who were Iranian citizens would not be deprived of their inheritance rights.[38]

The laws enacted and the decrees issued by the Ottoman government attempted to resolve through codification the long-standing problems of the estates of Iranians who died in the Ottoman Empire. Yet the issue of intermarriage had complicated the problem and focused attention on the possibility of immoveable property coming under foreign ownership.

38. BOA, M.V. 15–33, 2 Rebiyülevvel 1304 (29 November 1886); M.V. 17–34, 29 Cemaziyülevvel 1304 (23 February 1887).

This fact was certainly one of the reasons that an exemption was made to the 1869 Law of Ottoman Nationality in not allowing wives and male children the right to acquire Iranian citizenship. In the clearest exposition of the concern over the transfer of immovable property to foreigners, the Ottoman government declared in 1889 that if the deceased was an Iranian citizen it was the duty of the registry office of the Iranian Embassy to register and divide the movable goods *(emval-i menkul)* of the estate. The immovable property *(emval-i gayr-i menkule),* however, could only be divided among Ottoman citizens.[39]

One case from 1889 illustrates how the Cabinet resolved these cases. The case involved Fatma Zehra Hanım, whose father was originally an Iranian citizen. Her husband, Hacı İbrahim, also an Iranian, had died. Fatma Zehra Hanım had a son, İbrahim, who claimed to be an Iranian citizen. The Iranian Embassy attempted to prove the Iranian citizenship of the son and take control of the estate. The Cabinet found that Fatma Zehra Hanım's father Hüseyin Efendi had immigrated to Istanbul, accepted Ottoman citizenship, and married her mother Esma Hanım, who was an Ottoman citizen. The Cabinet stated:

> The rule in force is clearly confirmed in the *Ferman-ı 'Ali* dated 11 Rebiyülahir 1237 [Mahmud II's 1822 Supreme Mandate Prohibiting Marriage with Iranians] and [was] recently [confirmed] in the [1874] prohibition of marriage act. The statements of the Iranian Embassy that [these rules should] not be applied in this case, and the protest by the State of Iran on the publication [of the 1874 law] are not acceptable.[40]

The Cabinet ruled that Fatma Zehra Hanım and İbrahim were considered Ottoman citizens with rights to inherit the immovable property.

Throughout the remaining decades of the Ottoman Empire, the Cabinet and various ministries of the Ottoman government were presented with questions over the legality and enforcement of the prohibition

39. BOA, M.V. 40–46, 26 Cemaziyülahir 1306 (27 February 1889); M.V. 61–12, 15 Cemaziyülevvel 1308 (27 December 1890).

40. BOA, M.V. 40–46, 26 Cemaziyülahir 1306 (27 February 1889).

of marriage between Ottoman women and Iranian men; with requests for clarification of the citizenship status of the wives and children born from marriages with Iranians, and with clarification of the procedures for determining the proper distribution of the estates of Iranians.[41] The Iranian government continued to challenge the legality of the 1874 prohibition and Article 32 of the AAN. Although various legal advisors considered the possibility of annulling the prohibition, in the end they held that the laws were legal and that the wives and children were considered Ottoman citizens, irrespective of whether they had been married, or the children had been born, before or after the 1874 publication date of the prohibition of marriage law.

41. BOA, HR.HMŞ.İŞO 7–1/4, 3 Kanunuevvel 1302 (18 February 1885); HR.HMŞ.İŞO 7–1/4, 3 Kanunuevvel 1308 (15 December 1890); M.V. 119–74, 29 Cemaziyülahir 1326 (29 July 1908); DH.SN.THR 33–74, 16 Nisan 1328 (19 April 1912); DH.SN.THR 42–16, 13 Şaban 1330 (28 July 1912); Dahiliye Nezareti Hukuk Kısım Belgeleri (DH.H) 67–47, 17 Zilkade 1330 (28 October 1912); DH.H 67–47, 14 Şubat 1328 (26 February 1913); DH.İUM 19–23/5–75, 15 Mart 1336 (15 March 1920).

5

Continuity and Challenges to the Marriage Prohibition During the Transition from the Ottoman Empire to the Turkish Republic

DURING THE CONSTITUTIONAL PERIOD (1909–1918), the ruling Committee of Union and Progress (CUP) confronted the precariousness of security on the empire's borders, as the result of the arrival of thousands of Muslim and Jewish refugees and the outbreak of World War I. Even during this period of war and disintegration, Ottoman officials maintained the status quo with respect to Ottoman-Iranian marriages.[1] In 1913, for example, the Office of the Grand Vizier took up the question of whether the prohibition of marriages between Ottoman women and Iranian men was based on religious or national differences. Their decision clearly confirmed that both reasons were operational. First, the legal advisors remarked that the intention behind Mahmud II's 1822 decree was to prevent the spread of Shiʿism in the Ottoman state by prohibiting marriages to Iranians and persons of unknown lineage. Second, they noted that the Law Protecting the Prohibition of Marriage Between Iranians and Ottoman Citizens of 1874 had not made a distinction with

1. During the Constitutional period, the empire lost its remaining Balkan territories when the Greeks acquired Macedonia in 1913, when Albania declared independence during the Balkan wars, and when Austria-Hungary formally annexed Bosnia and Herzegovina. Greece also took Crete, and Italy occupied Libya and the Dodecanese Islands. By 1913, only the land from Eastern Thrace to Bulgaria remained a part of the empire's European territory.

respect to religion, and therefore the prohibition of marriage remained in force for all Ottoman citizens, Muslim and non-Muslim alike.[2] The exemption of sons born before the 1886 publication date of the AAN pertained only to military service. In all other matters, the children of these marriages were Ottoman citizens and were liable for taxation and other responsibilities to the state.[3]

By 1914, however, some of the legal advisers from the Office of the Grand Vizier began to consider, for the first time, the possibility of canceling the 1874 law. The impetus for these discussions was a request from the Ottoman Embassy in Tehran to determine what steps were necessary to enact a new law amending the 1874 prohibition. The legal advisers noted that, in proclaiming the 1874 law, the government had aimed at restricting the number of Iranian citizens and the expansion of Shiʿism in the Ottoman state, but that this plan had not been successful.[4] The advisers called for a meeting of Sunni and Shiʿi experts in order to adopt a plan that would be satisfactory to both governments. The advisers cautioned, however, that it was still necessary to prevent Iranians from flooding into Iraq in order to escape military service, and that it was likely there would be more Iranian citizens in the region should the prohibition be repealed and Ottoman women and their children be allowed to take Iranian citizenship. They proposed a new law whereby these marriages could be legalized without causing an increase in the Iranian population in Iraq. The law would legalize the marriages but continue to deny Ottoman women and their children the right to acquire Iranian citizenship. The male children would still be obligated to perform military service. While recognizing that the exclusion would be contrary to the 1869 Law of Ottoman Nationality, they nevertheless proposed the following draft law:

> Article 1. Marriages between Iranians and Ottoman women are not prohibited.

2. BOA, HR.HMŞ.İŞO 146-3, 17 Mart 1329 (20 March 1913).
3. BOA, HR.HMŞ.İŞO 146-3, 8 Nisan 1329 (21 April 1913).
4. BOA, HR.HMŞ.İŞO 7-1/4, 1 Receb 1332 (26 May 1914).

> Article 2. In order to protect the original citizenship of Ottoman women who marry Iranians, they do not acquire the citizenship of their husbands.
>
> Article 3. The [male] children who are born from Ottoman women married to Iranian men will be obliged for military service.
>
> Article 4. The law dated 25 Zilkade 1291 [7 October 1874] and all other laws and regulations contrary to the regulation of this law are annulled.
>
> Article 5. The Office of the Şeyhülislam and the Justice, Interior, and Foreign Ministries are authorized to carry out the regulations of this law.[5]

No immediate action was taken to adopt the draft law legalizing these marriages, and, as a result of events in the Iraqi provinces in 1914, it is probable that the political will did not exist to annul the 1874 law. The issue of the legalization of these marriages was overshadowed in November of 1914 when the British invaded and occupied portions of southern Iraq. The Shi'i legal scholars *(müctehids)* in the region, having become politically active against Iranian concessions to the British in the late nineteenth century, and, more recently, in support of the Iranian revolution of 1905 through 1911, were the most organized force opposing the British occupation. They had a strong, centralized leadership that immediately called for a jihad against the British. Although the *ulema* were somewhat successful in gathering thousands to their cause, they nevertheless failed to oust the British (Nakash 1994, 49, 60–61).

The CUP, concerned about recent losses of large Muslim populations in Libya and the Balkans, strengthened their resolve to hold on to the Iraqi provinces. They supported Shi'i opposition to the British and called for Sunni-Shi'i unity. In 1916, the Iranian Embassy again requested recognition of the Iranian citizenship of the children born from Ottoman-Iranian marriages who were living in the provinces. The legal advisers to the Office of the Grand Vizier, perhaps still under the illusion that the Iraqi provinces could be saved for the empire—even in the midst of the

5. Ibid. See appendix D.

First World War, reaffirmed that the prohibition was still in force since the proposed draft law for its cancellation had not been enacted. The children of these marriages were, therefore, still considered Ottoman citizens.[6] In 1917, the Office of the Grand Vizier, in fact, reversed its earlier recommendation to annul the prohibition, which had resulted in the draft law. In a discussion about the military tax *(bedel-i askeri),* the legal advisers clearly explained the motivation for the original prohibition and the need for its continuation:

> Following the Battle of Çaldıran [1514] up until the year 1200 [1785–1786], it was not possible for Iranians or other foreigners to reside at will in the Ottoman state. The Ottoman government [therefore] was not so concerned with this matter.
>
> One hundred years ago, starting from the middle of the reign of Sultan Selim III [1789–1807], a great change occurred in the political arena because of modern discoveries like the invention of the telegraph, transporting mail by land and sea, and especially the development of railroads and steamships, and administrative reforms. [As a result] the number of foreign citizens settling [in the Ottoman state] increased and Iranians increased the most in comparison with others. In the period of Mahmud II [1808–1839], the *ferman* dated 1 Rebiyülahir 1237 [5 January 1822] was issued because of the [increase] of marriages of Iranian citizens with Ottoman women.[7]

The advisers determined that there was no reason to annul the prohibition.

By 1920, the legal advisers to the Office of the Grand Vizier had reversed themselves once again and were recommending the abolition of the law prohibiting Ottoman-Iranian marriages. In arguing against the traditional religious basis of the prohibition (to prevent the increase of Shiʿism in the empire), they took a very strong stand in favor of the nation-state and recognized that the issue was now clearly one of nationality. They noted that, according to Islamic law, intermarriage between the sects

6. BOA, HR.HMŞ.İŞO 7-1/4, 20 Nisan 1332 (3 May 1916).
7. BOA, HR.HMŞ.İŞO 146-3, 4 Zilkade 1335 (22 August 1917).

was legal, so Sunni men could marry Shiʿi women, and Shiʿi men could marry Sunni women. The advisers stated that the original law prohibiting these marriages was intended to prevent the spread of Shiʿism and was enacted for political reasons so that the number of Iranian citizens in the Ottoman Empire would not multiply; but now, also for political reasons, it was necessary to abolish the law. Referring to the 1914 draft law, the advisers asserted that the law could clearly be written to ensure that Ottoman women married to Iranians, and their children, remained Ottoman citizens. The advisers accepted arguments from the Iranian Embassy as to why this law should be annulled. It was impossible, for example, to know the true numbers of Iranians living in the Ottoman state, so it was also impossible to know if their numbers were increasing. The advisors also argued that the prohibition did not have an effect on citizenship anyway. Ottoman women who went into exile because of these marriages nevertheless remained Ottoman citizens. In cases where Ottoman women returned to Ottoman territory and claimed Iranian citizenship, they and their children were still considered Ottoman citizens. It was clear, therefore, that the prohibition was useless because women who married Iranians and returned from exile were recognized by the government as Ottoman citizens. In the opinion of the advisers, it was time to annul the law.[8] In 1920, however, no action was taken to cancel the prohibition.

The prohibition remained in force after the proclamation of the first constitution of the Turkish Republic on 20 January 1921. In August of 1921, the Foreign Ministry asked permission from the Parliament to confirm the Iranian citizenship of several children who were born to non-Muslim Ottoman women. Even at this late date, the Parliament reaffirmed that the prohibition of marriages to Iranians was still in force and included all citizens, Muslim and non-Muslim alike.[9]

8. BOA, HR.HMŞ.İŞO 7-1/5, 12 Eylül (12 September 1920).

9. BOA, M.V. 221–268, 24 Zilhicce 1339 (29 August 1921). As an exception to their broad ruling, the Parliament decided that since this specific issue was limited to only a few persons, it was acceptable to consider these children Iranian citizens.

The legal basis for citizenship in Turkey was drawn from both the Law of Ottoman Nationality of 1869 and the Treaty of Peace signed in Lausanne on 24 July 1923 (Zürcher 2003, 167–70).[10] Turkish citizenship was based on the foundation of citizenship by territory *(jus soli)*, and Turkey, thereby, relinquished all rights over former Ottoman territories outside the borders of modern Turkey. Under Article 30 of Section II, "Nationality," the Treaty of Peace stated:

> Turkish subjects habitually resident in territory which in accordance with the provisions of the present Treaty is detached from Turkey will become *ipso facto* in the conditions laid down by the local law, nationals of the State to which such territory is transferred. (*League of Nations* 1924, 29; Davis 2000, 62–63)

Since Iraq was by treaty considered a nation separate from Ottoman territory, and the majority of the Shi'i population of the former Ottoman Empire no longer lived within the borders of modern Turkey, the prohibition of marriage between Ottoman women and Iranian men became an anachronism that was no doubt recognized as such by the Parliament. Without fanfare or explanatory memorandum, the Parliament finally passed the law of 26 April 1926 Concerning the Preservation of the Prohibition of Marriage Between Iranian and Turkish Citizens. The law contained five articles, which stated:

> Article 1. The prohibition concerning marriages of Iranians with Turkish women is abolished.
>
> Article 2. After this, all formalities that arise from these kinds of marriages are subject to public laws.

10. This treaty, an agreement between the British Empire, France, Italy, Japan, Greece, Romania, the Serb-Croat-Slovene State, and Turkey, was enacted after the cessation of hostilities in World War I and the subsequent Turkish struggle for independence. The negotiations between countries at Lausanne led to the abolishment of the sultanate and remaining Ottoman ministries in Istanbul, and the transfer of power to the Grand National Assembly and Mustafa Kemal in Ankara.

> Article 3. With respect to the rules in force as a result of the prohibition, all matters such as citizenship that have been concluded up until now are valid.
>
> Article 4. This law is valid from the date of publication.
>
> Article 5. Officials of the Ministries of Justice, Interior, and Foreign Affairs are commissioned to carry out the provisions of this law.[11]

By 1926, there was no need to uphold the prohibition because Iraq, having established a monarchy in 1921, was no longer a contested frontier.

The Treaty of Peace at Lausanne did, however, continue to uphold the law of dependent citizenship. Article 36 under Section II, "Nationality," stated:

> For the purposes of the provisions of this Section, the status of a married woman will be governed by that of her husband, and the status of children under eighteen years of age by that of their parents. (*League of Nations* 1924, 29)

Under the Law Concerning the Preservation of the Prohibition of Marriage Between Iranian and Turkish Citizens of 1926, Turkish women were finally allowed to legally marry Iranian citizens but, ironically, continued to be considered "dependents," whereby they lost their original citizenship and were required to adopt the nationality of their husbands; a bittersweet accomplishment, to be sure.

11. *Düstur.* 3. tertip, 7. cilt, İkinci bası, s. 873; *Resmi Ceride* (5 Mayıs 1926), Kanun No. 824; Unat 1966, 37.

6

Conclusion

THE PROHIBITION OF MARRIAGE between Ottoman women and Iranian men, enacted by law in 1874, was employed in this book as a framework and departure point to examine and analyze two larger issues of concern to scholars specializing in the history of the late Ottoman Empire. The first issue is the ways the idea of nationalism and citizenship entered into the empire, the meaning of these ideas in the Ottoman context, and the mechanisms used by officials to promote these concepts to create "national" loyalty to the dynastic state. This issue is particularly relevant for Ottoman historians of intellectual history who have examined the role of Ottomanism *(Osmanlılık)* in creating an Ottoman national ideal. These scholars have examined the development of Ottoman nationalism as an intellectual endeavor by the ruling elites, which was intended to unify the empire. As important as this scholarship has been for our understanding of the mechanisms used by the intellectual classes in addressing nineteenth-century trends toward nation-state and modernity, there is a void in the scholarship concerning the ways these concepts influenced official policies in the Tanzimat and post-Tanzimat periods.

The second major issue for consideration is center-periphery relations as represented by Ottoman official attitudes toward frontier regions. Official attitudes were most clearly reflected by centralization policies, which attempted to bring these territories under tighter control. As mentioned in the beginning of this book, the majority of recent studies on Ottoman frontier policies have focused on military campaigns, and economic, administrative, and educational development that created more efficient forms of bureaucratization and more effective mechanisms to exert tighter controls over these peripheral regions. We have examined the conceptual and institutional processes by which gender and personal status issues related to marriages between Ottoman women and Iranian men became an integral part of this centralizing process in the Iraqi frontier provinces and a way to analyze larger political, social, and cultural issues. As with most historical analysis that relies on archival sources, the documents have been the driving force behind this choice in perspective. The Ottoman determination to uphold this prohibition, which was so clearly and repeatedly delineated in these documents and case studies, leaves no doubt about the importance of the 1874 law to Ottoman centralization policies and control over the Iraqi provinces.

❧

It is useful to again consider Hugh Seton-Watson's theory of "official nationalism" in order to understand Ottoman official attitudes toward the concept of nationalism. As already noted, official nationalism was common among nineteenth-century dynastic powers, which attempted to create a merger between the nation and the dynastic empire. One of the main goals of the intellectuals who supported "Ottomanism" was to create an "official imperial nationalism" whose primary loyalty was to the royal family and which transcended more local religious and ethnic bonds. Tanzimat-era Ottomanism was perhaps most clearly elucidated by Fuad Paşa, the Ottoman foreign minister who in 1861 reaffirmed the hierarchical nature of the relationship between the dynasty and its subjects. In exchange for their loyalty to the sultan, Ottoman subjects would be treated with equality and equanimity. Nationalism during this period meant loyalty and obedience to the dynasty.

At the end of the nineteenth century, Sultan Abdülhamid II sought to reaffirm the legitimacy of the dynasty by overlaying "official imperial nationalism" with an emphasis on Islamic legitimacy in the person of the sultan and his role as caliph. Abdülhamid emphasized the fundamental dogma of the Hanafi School by sending teachers and *ulema* into the peripheries of the empire to teach the tenets of Sunni Islam and create a loyal population among disparate ethnicities and religious persuasions. His policies of expanding Sunni Islam were particularly evident in the Ottoman eastern provinces, where officials were concerned with the increase in Shi'ism. The meaning of official imperial nationalism became more fluid in the post-Hamidian period, as evinced in parliamentary discussions. As the empire lost its remaining territories in the Balkans, and entered into World War I, opportunities opened for more variations on the meaning of official imperial nationalism, and more challenges to the concept of Ottomanism as the only possible ideology for unifying the empire.

Official nationalism would appear to be nothing more than an intellectual exercise unless it was used in the service of policies that would carry out its goals of unifying an ethnically and religiously diverse population. In this respect, John Breuilly's emphasis on nationalism as a mechanism of power politics is especially relevant to the Ottoman experience. The official imperial nationalism of Ottomanism may be considered a political movement that sought to exercise state power, and justify that power, in the service of the extensive centralization policies put into place during the mid- to late nineteenth century. The interests and values of the centralizing state took priority over local concerns in the borderlands, such as the three eastern provinces of Ottoman Iraq.

Concomitant with Ottoman official nationalism as a ruling-class strategy, the Ottoman concept of citizenship was also a part of the centralizing monarchy's attempt to impose on its subjects a new order that would create social integration. Ottoman citizens were not demanding citizenship rights; on the contrary, the ruling elites were extending certain privileges and responsibilities to the population in order to strengthen the empire and centralize control over the peripheries. Reflecting on citizenship in 1861, Fuad Paşa maintained that subject-citizens were to be uncritically loyal to the sultan—an authoritarian but benevolent and modernizing power, who embodied the nation and who maintained stability, but treated each subject with compassion and justice. The clearest statement of Tanzimat-era citizenship was the Law of Ottoman Nationality of 1869. The law outlined basic rights and created a universal political identity based on residence and birth through the paternal line, which thereby allowed the government to designate who were legal residents and who were foreigners.

ര

For the Ottomans, control of the right to citizenship became an important component of its package of centralization policies, and an essential element in exerting its power over peripheral regions. One of the mechanisms they used to manage access to citizenship was through the regulation of marriage. As discussed in the introduction and throughout this book, marriage was intimately connected with social and economic life, and had an impact on Ottoman perceptions of public order in the eastern provinces. The Ottoman conception of gender relations did not diverge markedly from most nineteenth-century views of familial relations, which held that, for stability, the husband was the head of the household. In this model, the husband also carried the status of citizen and transferred that status to his wife and children. This was the concept of "dependent citizenship," which was almost universally applied in countries throughout the world. The wife, therefore, had no choice in terms of citizenship. Her duty was to support her husband's citizenship obligations, instill in her children loyalty to the state, and create a familial stability that would lead to stability of the nation.

Women's roles in transferring loyalty to the state to their children, as well as loyalty of the family to the state, clearly underpinned the ideology behind the 1874 law prohibiting marriages between Ottoman women and Iranian men. The law was promulgated specifically to control and potentially reduce the number of Shiʿites in the frontier provinces of Basra, Baghdad, and Mosul. These provinces had societies that were ethnically, culturally, and religiously distinct from the center and had for many years remained outside of central control. The Iraqi provinces had their own institutions of governance that resisted Ottoman attempts at centralization. Control of the provinces was difficult because of their distance from the center of power and because of the role they played as a backdrop to the Shiʿi-Sunni conflict. This zone was, additionally, marked throughout the period of empires by an Ottoman-Iranian contest for political, religious, social, and economic influence and control.

The demographic importance of marriage becomes evident when examining Ottoman policies for the frontier provinces of Iraq. Ottoman attempts to bring the provinces under the control of the central administration were directly connected to geopolitical realities that centered on the centuries-long rivalry between Ottoman and Iranian leaders and Sunni-Shiʿi hostility. In the construction of citizenship in the mid–nineteenth century, the Ottomans took into account both historical and contemporary geopolitical exigencies, and they legislated citizenship rights to reflect these realities. Officials believed that Shiʿism was increasing among the population and seriously threatening the government's control over the provinces. In an attempt to stop this increase, the Ottoman government enacted the 1874 prohibition, a measure that they believed would consolidate Ottoman control over the provinces in a number of ways: maintaining the loyalty of the population, decreasing the number of soldiers in the Sixth Army who were suspected of being Shiʿa, and also preventing the material wealth of the empire from falling into the hands of Iranian citizens.

The government was clearly attempting to control women's biological choices by limiting the number of children who would be considered Iranian citizens and Shiʿites as the result of taking the citizenship and religion of their Iranian fathers. Government policies toward Sunni Islam were intended also to increase the numbers of Sunni-born children and thereby create the desired religious dominance in the provinces. Government policies forbidding Ottoman-Iranian marriages forced upon women the obligation to support Sunni dominance by contracting only marriages that were considered legal under the exemption to Ottoman citizenship law.

These Ottoman policies were concomitant with the realization that, in order to secure its borders, the government needed to create and maintain its population's loyalty to the state. The demographic aspect of marriage was important to Ottoman frontier policies because women and their choice of husbands were intimately linked to these domestic and geopolitical policies. First, Ottoman policies attempting to control the reproductive choices of their female citizens placed women in the role of the "biological reproducers" of the Ottoman-Sunni society. Ottoman women's bodies were legally co-opted by government restrictions over marriage partners, which were intended to limit the number of undesirables (Shiʿites). Second, women were the reproducers of the boundaries of ethnic, religious, and national groups. The Ottoman marriage prohibition was targeted primarily toward its eastern provinces and placed women in the position of maintaining religious, ethnic, and social norms appropriate to the Ottoman-Sunni state. Third, women were considered symbolic markers of the nation and of Ottoman cultural identity. Women reinforced Ottoman culture by conveying the language, rituals, and myths of the culture to their children, who would, as a result, remain loyal to the Ottoman state. Fourth, in the nineteenth century, women were at the center of the ancient struggles between the Sunnis and Shi'ites and between Ottomans and Iranians. Women, in their choice of marriage partners, were participants in the national, economic, political, and military struggles between the Ottomans and Iranians in the Ottoman eastern provinces. All of these factors highlight how the Ottoman policy was particularly important in frontier regions where women (and the nation) needed to be protected against invasion and violation of its boundaries (by Iranians and the Iranian state).

ꕥ

The usefulness analyzing this law in investigating larger processes can be further seen when we consider a number of factors. This 1874 prohibition was the only exclusion to the international standard of "dependent citizenship," which was the foundation of the 1869 Law of Ottoman Nationality. The nationality law was a wholesale adoption of French law with respect to dependent citizenship, but the law was adapted by the enactment of this exclusionary 1874 law to control the Iraqi border provinces.

The prohibition persisted in the face of confusions and challenges throughout the last fifty years of the empire. Case records of the Ottoman Cabinet and various ministies discussed in this book indicate confusion among Ottoman provincial officials. Many petitions reached central governing institutions requesting confirmation that the prohibition remained in force. Such requests evince the fact the Ottoman women continued to marry Iranian men and that the 1874 law was ineffective in preventing these marriages from being contracted.

Petitions from various provinces asked whether non-Muslim Ottomans were included in the prohibition, and whether Sunni and non-Muslim Iranians were also to be included. Contradictory opinions on these questions from the legal advisors to the various ministries created further confusion for provincial officials. Throughout these last fifty years, difficulties also remained in determining the military status of children whose parents claimed Iranian citizenship in Iraqi provinces—irrespective of the many conscription laws that were meant to clarify this issue. All of these petitions from provincial officials fundamentally highlight the impossibility of legislating and enforcing a law that attempted to regulate Ottoman women's choice of marriage partners.

The 1874 law also endured continual opposition from the Iranian government, and the presentation of a draft law from the legal advisers to the Office of the Grand Vizier that would legalize Ottoman-Iranian marriages while still maintaining control over the citizenship status of Ottoman women and their children.

The Ottoman government inserted its authority into this personal status issue because officials recognized that Ottoman-Iranian marriages had an impact on social and economic life in ways that compromised direct Ottoman control over this indispensable frontier region. The documents discussed in this book clearly reveal that the marriage prohibition was considered an essential strategy in controlling the increase of Shiʿism in the province. If the prohibition was annulled and the marriages legalized, then, according to international standards of dependent citizenship, Ottoman women and their children would lose their Ottoman citizenship and become Iranian citizens. If these marriages were permitted, then officials feared that many Ottoman-Sunni women would convert to Shiʿism and take Iranian citizenship, and many children would be born into Shi ʿism and take the Iranian citizenship of their fathers. Such an occurrence would only increase concerns over the loyalty of the provinces' population to the Ottoman state. The loyalty of the male Shiʿi children would also be doubtful, since they would compose the bulk of the armed forces, whose integrity could be compromised. Finally, with respect to inheritance, Ottoman women and their children had to be counted as Ottoman citizens for the sake of keeping real estate in the hands of Ottoman citizens. If these marriages were permitted, a large amount of territory could be transferred into the hands of Iranian citizens upon the death of Iranian fathers.

Nation-building has often been based on controlling the status of women and their children. In the nineteenth century, when the Ottoman Empire began adopting European juridical and administrative models, it imported an idea of citizenship with respect to marriage that did not allow for women's agency in the question of their citizenship. The government bent citizenship rights to the requirements of geopolitical exigencies. It inscribed in the particularities of the law restrictions on women's marriage partners, thereby subordinating women's citizenship to the state's needs. Ironically, the European concept of citizenship at that time permitted discrimination against women in the matter of marriage, because European law required that married women accept the citizenship of their husbands. This law fit neatly with existing Ottoman patriarchal structures, with only one exception—an exception that highlights the difficulty confronting the Ottoman Empire in establishing policies that established effective control of all its citizens. The social and legal dynamics contrasted in this book illustrate the ambiguity and complexities inherent in the Ottoman approach to developing a working form of nationalism and citizenship that they could effectively apply to their easternmost frontier provinces.

Appendix A

Appendix B

Appendix C

Appendix D

Appendix E

References

Index

APPENDIX A

Supreme Mandate (Buyruldu-ı 'Ali) *Concerning the Prohibition of Marriage with Iranians of 5 January 1822*

All Muslims are obliged to know the religion of Islam and to learn matters concerning belief, but some people of ignorance who deviate from these obligatory principles marry, or cause [others] to marry, by undertaking acts not suitable to the dogma of religious precepts and the sacred observance of Islam. [If] people of ignorance change Muslims schools, may God forbid, [they] will be subject to disappointment in this world and the next.

In the matter of contracting marriages to persons of unknown lineage, most sons and grandsons cannot inquire into the origins of their descendants. [Therefore] it is the obligation of the neighborhood imam, who is making the contract, to make the marriage contract free from doubt by investigating the family origins of the person, in order not to go against the beloved Islamic faith, or to be surprised by making marriage contracts between persons of unknown origins and sect.

Also, in this matter, those who contract, or cause to contract, marriage between Sunni women and Iranians will be investigated and, when it is proven, [will be] arrested.

From this time onward, as a consequence of this matter, the religious authorities of Istanbul and environs who absolutely do not investigate, or are negligent and do not pay attention; the neighborhood imams, also, who give permission, who contract marriage, or who dare to cause this to occur and allow people to marry [persons] who are inclined to ignorance, Shi'a, heretics, persons of unknown lineage, and Iranians, will be punished with the strongest punishments.

For the *kadılar* of Istanbul, Eyüp, and Üsküdar, the matter of the Imperial Decree is clear. The neighborhood imams, who perform marriages in these categories, will be strongly punished. The strongest punishment is declared [also] for those who give and take girls to these persons of unknown lineage, and may God forbid situations like this, henceforth.

APPENDIX B

Law of Ottoman Nationality of 19 January 1869

Article 1. Persons born at a time when their parents or only [their] father are of Ottoman nationality are considered Ottoman subjects.

Article 2. Any person born in the imperial dominions [Ottoman Empire] at a time when his [or her] parents are of foreign nationality can, by right, within three years, beginning with the date of his [or her] majority, claim Ottoman nationality.

Article 3. A foreigner of age who has lived in the Ottoman Empire consecutively for five years can obtain Ottoman nationality by submitting personally, or through an intermediary, a petition to the Department of Foreign Affairs.

Article 4. The Imperial Ottoman Government extraordinarily receives into its allegiance foreigners as well whom it considers to be worthy of an exceptional favor, even should they not have fulfilled the condition prescribed in the preceding article.

Article 5. Persons who, being authorized, enter from Ottoman into a foreign nationality are, from the date when they changed their nationality, considered as foreign subjects and treated as such. But if he should enter into a foreign nationality without being authorized by the Imperial Ottoman Government, his new nationality shall be considered as null and void, and he shall be considered as an Ottoman subject as before, and in every matter he shall be treated exactly as Ottoman subjects are treated. In any case, the abandonment by an Ottoman subject of his nationality depends on an instrument to be granted in virtue of an imperial *irade* (decree).

Article 6. If the Ottoman Empire should so wish it can reject from its subjection the person who, without authorization from the Imperial Ottoman Government, changes his nationality in a foreign country, or enters into the military service of a foreign government. The return into the imperial dominions of persons of this category whose nationality has been rejected is forbidden.

Article 7. The woman who, while an Ottoman subject, marries a foreigner may return to her original nationality if, within three years following the date of her husband's death, she petitions for it. The provision of this article applies to the person. The matter of ownership of *mülk* and *arazi* property is subject to the general laws and regulations.

Article 8. A child, even if he should be minor, of an Ottoman subject who has been naturalized abroad or has lost his nationality does not follow the condition of his father but remains an Ottoman subject. A child, even if he should be a minor, of an alien who has been naturalized in Turkey does not follow the condition of his father and remains an alien.

Article 9. Every person inhabiting the imperial dominions is considered as an Ottoman subject and treated as an Ottoman subject. If he is a foreign subject it is necessary for him to prove it in a regular manner.

APPENDIX C

Law Protecting the Prohibition of Marriage Between Iranians and Ottoman Citizens of 7 October 1874

Article 1. Marriages between Ottoman and Iranian citizens, as in olden times, are strongly prohibited.

Article 2. Those [officials] who are authorized to perform marriages and who act against the prohibition will be held responsible.

Article 3. [If] a woman who is an Ottoman citizen marries someone who is an Iranian citizen against the prohibition, both the woman and her children will be considered Ottoman citizens and liable for conscription, military tax, and all other financial obligations.

APPENDIX D

Draft Law Concerning the Prohibition of Marriage Between Ottoman Women and Iranian Men of 26 May 1914

Article 1. Marriages between Iranians and Ottoman women are not prohibited.

Article 2. In order to protect the original citizenship of Ottoman women who marry Iranians, they do not acquire the citizenship of their husbands.

Article 3. The [male] children who are born from Ottoman women married to Iranian men will be obliged for military service.

Article 4. The law dated 25 Zilkade 1291 [7 October 1874] and all other laws and regulations contrary to the regulation of this law are annulled.

Article 5. The Office of the Şeyhülislam and the Justice, Interior and Foreign Ministries are authorized to carry out the regulations of this law.

APPENDIX E

Law Concerning the Preservation of the Prohibition of Marriage Between Iranian and Turkish Citizens of 26 April 1926

Article 1. The prohibition concerning marriages of Iranians with Turkish women is abolished.

Article 2. After this, all formalities that arise from these kinds of marriages are subject to public laws.

Article 3. With respect to the rules in force as a result of the prohibition, all matters such as citizenship that have been concluded up until now are valid.

Article 4. This law is valid from the date of publication.

Article 5. Officials of the Ministries of Justice, Interior, and Foreign Affairs are commissioned to carry out the provisions of this law.

References

Archives

Başbakanlık Osmanlı Arşivi (BOA)
Dahiliye Nezareti Hukuk Kısım Belgeleri (DH.H)
Dahiliye Nezareti Hukuk Müşavirliği Belgeleri (DH.HMŞ)
Dahiliye Nezareti İdari Kısım Belgeleri (DH.İD)
Dahiliye Nezareti İdare-i Umumiye Belgeleri (DH.İUM)
Dahiliye Nezareti Mebani-i Emiriye ve Hapishaneler Müdüriyeti Belgeleri (DH.MB.HPS.M)
Dahiliye Nezareti Muhaberat-ı Umumiye İdaresi Belgeleri (DH.MUİ)
Dahiliye Nezareti Sicill-i Nüfus İdare-i Umumiyesi Belgeleri (Tahrirat Kalemi) (DH.SN.THR)
Dahiliye Nezareti Siyasi Kısım Belgeleri (DH.SYS)
Ecnebi Defterleri
Hoover Institution Archives, Hidayet Dağdeviren Collection (HIA-HDC)
Hukuk Muşavirliği İştişare Odası (HR.HMŞ.İŞO)
İrade Dahiliye
İrade Hariciye
İrade Hususi
İrade Meclis-i Mahsus
Meclis-i Vükela Mazbataları (M.V.)
Sadaret Mektubi Kalemi Mühimme Kalemi Odası Belgeleri (A.MKT.MHM)
Yıldız Mütenevvi Maruzat Evrakı (Y.MTV)
Yıldız Sadaret Hususı Maruzat Evrakı (Y.A.HUS)
Yıldız Sadaret Resmi Maruzat Evrakı (Y.A.RES)

Other Primary Sources

Ceride-i Mehakim
Düstur

Resmi Ceride
Takvim-i Velayi

Books, Articles, Periodicals, Dissertations, and Papers

Abu Husayn, Abdul-Rahim. 1993. "The Shiites in Lebanon and the Ottomans in the 16th and 17th Centuries." In *Convegno Sul Tema La Shi'a Nell'Impero Ottomano,* Roma, 15 April 1991, 107–19. Rome: Accademia Nazionale Dei Lincei, Fondazione Leone Caetani.

Abu-Manneh, Butrus. 1990. "The Sultan and the Bureaucracy: The Anti-Tanzimat Concepts of Grand Vizier Mahmud Nedim Pasa." *IJMES* 22, no. 3:257–74.

Ahmad, Feroz. 1984. "The State and Intervention in Turkey." *Turcica* 16:51–64.

———. 2000. "Ottoman Perceptions of the Capitulations 1800–1914." *Journal of Islamic Studies* 11, no. 1:1–20.

Aitchison, C. U. 1909. *A Collection of Treaties, Engagements and Sanads, Relating to India and Neighboring Countries.* Vol. 7, *Containing the Treaties, etc., Relating to Persia, the Arab Principalities in the Persian Gulf and Oman.* Calcutta: Superintendent of Government Printing.

Akarlı, Engin. 1990. "The Defense of the Libyan Provinces, 1882–1888." In *Studies on Ottoman Diplomatic History, The Ottomans and Africa,* vol. 5, edited by Sinan Kuneralp and Selim Deringil, 75–85. Istanbul: Isis Press.

———. 1993. *The Long Peace: Ottoman Lebanon, 1861–1920.* London: I.B. Tauris.

Akiba, Jun. 2007. "Preliminaries to a Comparative History of the Russian and Ottoman Empires: Perspectives from Ottoman Studies." In *Imperiology: From Imperial Knowledge to Discussing the Russian Empire,* edited by Kimitaka Matsuzato, 33–47. Sapporo: Slavic Research Center, 21st Century COE Program Slavic Eurasian Studies.

Altunsu, Dr. Abdülkadir. 1972. *Osmanlı Şeyhülislamları.* Ankara: Ayyıldız Matbaası.

Amirpur, Katajun. 2005. "The Changing Approach to the Text: Iranian Scholars and the Quran." *MES* 41, no. 3:337–50.

Anderson, Benedict. 1994. *Imagined Communities. Reflections on the Origin and Spread of Nationalism.* London: Verso.

Anscombe, Frederick F. 1997. *The Ottoman Gulf: The Creation of Kuwait, Saudi Arabia, and Qatar.* New York: Columbia Univ. Press.

Anthias, Floya, and Nira Yuval-Davis. 1989. "Introduction." In *Women-Nation-State,* edited by Nira Yuval-Davis, Floya Anthias, and Jo Campling, 1–15. London: Macmillan.

Arat, Yeşim. 2000. "Gender and Citizenship in Turkey." In *Gender and Citizenship in the Middle East,* edited by Suad Joseph, 275–86. Syracuse: Syracuse Univ. Press.

Augustine-Adams, Kif. 2002. "'She Consents Implicitly': Women's Citizenship, Marriage, and Liberal Political Theory in Late-Nineteenth- and Early-Twentieth-Century Argentina." *Journal of Women's History* 13, no. 4:8–30.

Aybay, Rona. 1980. *Kadının Uyrukluğu Üzerinde Evlenmenin Etkisi.* Ankara: Ankara Üniversitesi Siyasal Bilgiler Fakültesi Yayınları, no. 450.

Al-Baghdadi, 'Abd al-Kathir ibn-Tahir. 1919. *Al-Fark bain al-Firak.* In *Moslem Schisms and Sects, Part I.* Translated by Kate Chambers Seelye. New York: Columbia Univ. Press.

Al-Baghdadi, 'Abd al-Kathir ibn-Tahir. 1935. *Al-Fark bain al-Firak.* In *Moslem Schisms and Sects, Part II.* Translated by Abraham S. Halkin. Tel Aviv: Palestine Publishing Co., Ltd.

Baljon, J. M. S. 1968. *Modern Muslim Koran Interpretation (1880–1960).* Leiden, The Netherlands: E. J. Brill.

Behar, Cem. 2004. "Neighborhood Nuptials: Islamic Personal Law and Local Customs—Marriage Records in a *Mahalle* of Traditional Istanbul (1864–1907)." *IJMES* 36, no. 4:537–59.

Behar, Moshe. 2005. "Do Comparative and Regional Studies of Nationalism Intersect?" *IJMES* 37, no. 4:587–612.

Bein, Amit. 2006. "Politics, Military Conscription, and Religious Education in the Late Ottoman Empire." *IJMES* 38, no. 2:283–301.

Berkes, Niyazi. 1964. *The Development of Secularism in Turkey.* Montreal: McGill Univ. Press.

Bhabha, Homi. 1994. "Of Mimicry and Man: The Ambivalence of Colonial Discourse." In *The Location of Culture,* edited by Homi Bhabha, 121–31. New York: Routledge.

Blumi, Isa. 2003a. "Beyond the Margins of Empire: Issues Concerning Ottoman Boundaries in Yemen and Albania." In *MIT Electronic Journal of Middle East Studies. Crossing Boundaries: New Perspectives on the Middle East,* edited by Thomas Kühn, 18–26. Accessed at http://web.mit.edu/cis/www/mitejmes/ (discontinued).

———. 2003b. "Contesting the Edges of the Ottoman Empire: Rethinking Ethnic and Sectarian Boundaries in the Malësore, 1878–1912." *IJMES* 35, no. 2:237–56.

Bosworth, C. Edmund. 1993. "Baha' al-Din al-'Amili in the Two Worlds of the Ottomans and Safavids." In *Convegno Sul Tema La Shi'a Nell'Impero Ottomano,* Roma, 15 April 1991, 85–105. Rome: Accademia Nazionale Dei Lincei, Fondazione Leone Caetani.

Bozkurt, Gülnihal. 1989. *Gayrimüslim Osmanlı Vatandaşlarının Hukuki Durumu (1839–1914).* Ankara: Türk Tarih Kurumu Basımevi.

Bredbenner, Candice. 1998. *A Nationality of Her Own.* Berkeley: Univ. of California Press.

Breuilly, John. 1982. *Nationalism and the State.* New York: St. Martin's Press.

Butenschon, Nils A., Uri Davis, and Manuel Hassassian, eds. 2000. *Citizenship and the State in the Middle East: Approaches and Applications.* Syracuse: Syracuse Univ. Press.

Buzpınar, Ş. Turfan. 1996. "Opposition to the Ottoman Caliphate in the Early Years of Abdulhamid II: 1877–82." *Die Welt des Islams* 36, no. 1:59–89.

Calmard, J. 1989. "'Azadari." *EI,* vol. 3, edited by Ehsan Yarshater, 174–77. London: Routledge and Kegan Paul.

Camiscioli, Elisa. 1999. "Intermarriage, Independent Nationality, and the Individual Rights of French Women, the Law of 10 August 1927." *French Politics, Culture, and Society* 17, nos. 3–4:52–75.

Çetinsaya, Gökhan. 2006. *Ottoman Administration of Iraq, 1890–1908.* London and New York: Routledge.

Christophoros, Psilos. 2006. "Albanian Nationalism and Unionist Ottomanization, 1908 to 1912." *Mediterranean Quarterly* 17, no. 3:26–42.

Cleveland, William L. 1985. *Islam Against the West: Shakib Arslan and the Campaign for Arab Nationalism.* Austin: Univ. of Texas Press.

Cole, Juan R. I. 1986. "'Indian Money' and the Shi'i Shrine Cities of Iraq, 1786–1850." *MES* 22, no. 4:461–80.

Cole, Juan R. I., and Moouan Momen. 1986. "Mafia, Mob and Shi'ism in Iraq: The Rebellion of Ottoman Karbala', 1824–1843." *Past and Present* 112:112–43.

Cronin, Stephanie. 1997. *The Army and the Creation of the Pahlavi State in Iran, 1910–1926.* London: I.B. Tauris.

Dahbour, Omar, and Micheline R. Ishay, eds. 1995. *The Nationalism Reader.* Atlantic Highlands, N.J.: Humanities Press International, Inc.

Danişmend, İsmail Hami. 1972. *İzahlı Osmanlı Tarihi Kronolojisi.* Vol. 4. Istanbul: Türkiye Yayınevi.

Davis, Uri. 2000. "Conceptions of Citizenship in the Middle East. State, Nation, and People." In *Citizenship and the State in the Middle East: Approaches and Applications,* edited by Nils A. Butenschon, Uri Davis, and Manuel Hassassian, 49–69. Syracuse: Syracuse Univ. Press.

Dawn, Ernest C. 1991. "Origins of Arab Nationalism." In *The Origins of Arab Nationalism,* edited by Rashid Khalidi, Lisa Anderson, Muhammad Muslih, and Reeva Simon, 3–26. New York: Columbia Univ. Press.

Deringil, Selim. 1990. "The Struggle Against Shiism in Hamidian Iraq. A Study in Ottoman Counter-Propaganda." *Die Welt des Islams* 30:45–62.

———. 1993. "The Invention of Tradition as Public Image in the Late Ottoman Empire, 1808 to 1908." *CSSH* 35:3–29.

———. 1998. *The Well-Protected Domains. Ideology and the Legitimation of Power in the Ottoman Empire, 1876–1909.* London: I.B. Tauris.

———. 2003. "'They Live in a State of Nomadism and Savagery': The Late Ottoman Empire and the Post-Colonial Debate." *CSSH* 45, no. 2:311–42.

Donner, Fred M. 1986. "The Formation of the Islamic State." *JAOS* 106, no. 2:283–96.

Douwes, Dick. 1999. "Reorganizing Violence: Traditional Recruitment Patterns and Resistance Against Conscription in Ottoman Syria." In *Arming the State: Military Conscription in the Middle East and Central Asia, 1775–1925,* edited by Erik J. Zürcher, 111–27. London: I.B. Tauris.

Duben, Alan, and Cem Behar. 1991. *Istanbul Households. Marriage, Family and Fertility, 1880–1940.* Cambridge: Cambridge Univ. Press.

Duguid, Stephen. 1973. "The Politics of Unity: Hamidian Policy in Eastern Anatolia." *MES* 9, no. 2:139–55.

Düzdağ, M. Ertuğrul. 1983. *Şeyhülislam Ebussuud Efendi Fetvaları Isığında 16. Asır Türk Hayatı.* Istanbul: Enderun Kitabevi.

Eberhard, Elke. 1970. *Osmanische Polemik gegen die Safawiden im 16. Jahrhundert nach arabischen Handschriften.* Freiburg, Germany: Klaus Schwarz.

Ende, Werner. 1997. "The Nakhāwila, a Shiite Community in Medina Past and Present." *Die Welt des Islams,* new series, 37, no. 3, *Shiites and Sufis in Saudi Arabia,* 267–91.

Fahmy, Khaled. 1999. "The Navy and Its Deserters: Conscription in Mehmed Ali's Egypt." In *Arming the State: Military Conscription in the Middle East and Central Asia, 1775–1925,* edited by Erik J. Zürcher, 59–77. London: I.B. Tauris.

Falk, Richard. 1994. "The Making of Global Citizenship." In *The Condition of Citizenship,* edited by Bart van Steenbergen, 127–40. London: Sage Publications.

Farah, Caesar E. 1995/96. "Reassessing Sultan Abdülhamid II's Islamic Policy." *Archivum Ottomanicum* 14:191–212.

Faroqhi, Suraiya. 1994. *Pilgrims and Sultans. The Hajj under the Ottomans, 1517–1683.* London: I.B. Tauris.

Fattah, Hala. 1997. *The Politics of Regional Trade in Iraq, Arabia, and the Gulf, 1745–1900.* New York: State Univ. of New York Press.

Findley, Carter. 1980. *Bureaucratic Reform in the Ottoman Empire. The Sublime Porte, 1789–1922.* Princeton, N.J.: Princeton Univ. Press.

Finkel, Caroline. 2005. *Osman's Dream: The History of the Ottoman Empire.* New York: Basic Books.

Fleischer, Cornell. 1983. "Royal Authority, Dynastic Cyclism, and `Ibn Khaldunism' in Sixteenth-Century Ottoman Letters." *Journal of Asian and African Studies* 18, nos. 3–4:198–220.

Flournoy, Richard W. Jr., and Manley O. Hudson, eds. 1929. *A Collection of Nationality Laws of Various Countries as Contained in Constitutions, Statutes and Treaties.* New York: Oxford Univ. Press.

Fortna, Benjamin C. 2002. *Imperial Classroom: Islam, the State, and Education in the Late Ottoman Empire.* Oxford: Oxford Univ. Press.

Glassen, Erika. 1993. "Muharram Ceremonies ('Azadari) in Istanbul at the End of the XIXth and the Beginning of the XXth Century." In *Les Iraniens D'Istanbul,* edited by T. Zarcone and F. Zarinebaf-Shahr, 113–29. IFÉA/IFRI, Istanbul-Tehran.

Gölpınarlı, Abdülbaki. 1955. "Kızıl-baş." In *İslam Ansiklopedisi,* vol. 6, 789–95. Istanbul: Maarif Basımevi.

Gordon, Daniel. 2003. "Citizenship." *Encyclopedia of the Enlightenment,* edited by Alan Charles Kor, 241–47. Oxford: Oxford Univ. Press.

Habermas, Jürgen. 1994. "Citizenship and National Identity." In *The Condition of Citizenship,* edited by Bart van Steenbergen, 20–35. London: Sage Publications.

Halkin, Abrahim S. 1935. *Moslem Schisms and Sects.* Part 2. Tel Aviv: Palestine Publishing Co., Ltd.

Hanagan, Michael, and Charles Tilly, eds. 1999. *Extending Citizenship, Reconfiguring States.* Lanham, Md.: Rowman & Littlefield.

Hanioğlu, M. Şükrü. 1995. *The Young Turks in Opposition.* Oxford: Oxford Univ. Press.

———. 2001. *Preparation for a Revolution: The Young Turks, 1902–1908.* Oxford: Oxford Univ. Press.

Hanssen, Jens, Thomas Philipp and Stefan Weber. 2002. *The Empire in the City: Arab Provincial Capitals in the Late Ottoman Empire.* Beirut: Ergon Verlag Würzburg in Kommission.

Head-König, Anne-Lise. 1993. "Forced Marriages and Forbidden Marriages in Switzerland: State Control of the Formation of Marriage in Catholic and Protestant Cantons in the Eighteenth and Nineteenth Centuries." *Continuity and Change* 8, no. 3:441–65.

Helman, Sara. 2000. "Rights and Duties, Citizens and Soldiers. Conscientious Objection and the Redefinition of Citizenship in Israel." In *Citizenship and the State in the Middle East: Approaches and Applications,* edited by Nils A. Butenschon, Uri Davis, and Manuel Hassassian, 316–37. Syracuse: Syracuse Univ. Press.

Herslet, Sir Edward. 1891. *Treaties etc. Concluded Between Great Britain and Persia and Other Powers, Wholly or Partially in Force on the 1st April, 1891.* London: Butterworths.

Heuer, Jennifer. 2005. *The Family and the Nation: Gender and Citizenship in Revolutionary France, 1789–1830.* Ithaca, N.Y.: Cornell Univ. Press.

Hurewitz, Jacob Coleman, ed. 1975. *The Middle East and North Africa in World Politics: A Documentary Record.* Vol. 1, *European Expansion, 1535–1914.* New Haven, Conn.: Yale Univ. Press.

Imber, C. H. 1979. "The Persecution of Ottoman Shi'ites According to the *Mühimme Defterleri,* 1565–1585." *Der Islam* 56:245–73.

İnalcık, Halil. 1973. "Application of the Tanzimat and Its Social Effects." *Archivum Ottomanicum* 5:97–127.

İslamoğlu, Huri. 2000. "Property as a Contested Domain: A Reevaluation of the Ottoman Land Code of 1858." In *New Perspectives on Property and Land in the Middle East,* edited by Roger Owen, 3–61. Cambridge, Mass.: Harvard Univ. Press.

Al-Izzi, Khalid. 1972. *The Shatt al-Arab River Dispute in Terms of Law.* Baghdad: Ministry of Information, al-Huriyah Printing House.

Janowitz, Morris. 1980. "Observations on the Sociology of Citizenship: Obligations and Rights." *Social Forces* 59, no. 1:1–24.

Jansen, J. J. G. 1974. *The Interpretation of the Koran in Modern Egypt.* Leiden, The Netherlands: E. J. Brill.

Joseph, Suad, ed. 2000. *Gender and Citizenship in the Middle East.* Syracuse: Syracuse Univ. Press.

Judson, Pieter M. 1996. "The Gendered Politics of German Nationalism in Austria, 1880–1900." In *Austrian Women in the Nineteenth and Twentieth Centuries,* edited by David F. Good, Margarite Grandner, and Mary Jo Maynes, 1–17. Providence, R.I. and Oxford, England: Berghahn Books.

Karl, Rebecca E. 1998. "Creating Asia: China in the World at the Beginning of the Twentieth Century." *AHR* 103, no. 4:1096–118.

Karpat, Kemal. 2001. *The Politicization of Islam: Reconstructing Identity, State, Faith, and Community in the Late Ottoman State.* Oxford: Oxford Univ. Press.

———. 2002. *Studies on Ottoman Social and Political History. Selected Articles and Essays.* Leiden, The Netherlands: E. J. Brill.

Khadduri, Majid. 1955. *War and Peace in the Law of Islam.* Baltimore, Md.: Johns Hopkins Univ. Press.

Khoury, Dina Rizk. 1997. *State and Provincial Society in the Ottoman Empire. Mosul, 1540–1834.* Cambridge: Cambridge Univ. Press.

Kılıç, Dr. Remzi. 2001. *XVI. ve XVII. Yüzyıllarda Osmanlı-İran Siyasi Antlaşmaları.* Istanbul: Tez Yayınları.

Klein, Janet. 2007. "Kurdish Nationalists and Non-nationalist Kurdists: Rethinking Minority Nationalism and the Dissolution of the Ottoman Empire, 1908–1909." *Nations and Nationalism* 13, no. 1:135–53.

Köksal Yonca. 2008. "Rethinking Nationalism: State Projects and Community Networks in 19th-Century Ottoman Empire." *American Behavioral Scientist* 51, no. 10:1498–515.

Kühn, Thomas. 2002. "Ordering the Past of Ottoman Yemen, 1871–1914." *Turcica* 34:189–220.

———. 2003a. "An Imperial Borderland as Colony: Knowledge Production and the Elaboration of Difference in Ottoman Yemen, 1872–1919." *MIT Electronic Journal of Middle East Studies. Crossing Boundaries: New Perspectives on the Middle East,* vol. 3, edited by Thomas Kühn, 5–17. Accessed at http://web.mit.edu/cis/www/mitjmes/ (discontinued).

———, ed. 2003b. *MIT Electronic Journal of Middle East Studies. Crossing Boundaries: New Perspectives on the Middle East,* vol. 3. Accessed at http://web.mit.edu/cis/www/mitjmes/ (discontinued).

Kuran, Ercümend. 1968. "The Impact of Nationalism on the Turkish Elite in the Nineteenth Century." In *Beginnings of Modernization in the Middle East,* edited by William R. Polk and Richard L. Chambers, 109–17. Chicago: Univ. of Chicago Press.

Kütükoğlu, Bekir. 1975. "Les Relations Entre L'Empire Ottoman et L'Iran Dans La Seconde Moitié Du XVIe Siècle." *Turcica* 6:128–45.

———. 1993. *Osmanlı-İran Siyasi Münasebetleri (1578–1612).* Istanbul: İstanbul Fetih Cemiyeti.

Lamar, Howard, and Leonard Thompson. 1981. "Comparative Frontier History." In *The Frontier in History: North America and Southern Africa Compared,* edited by Howard Lamar and Leonard Thompson, 3–13. New Haven, Conn.: Yale Univ. Press.

Lambton, Ann K. S. 1981. *State and Government in Medieval Islam.* Oxford: Oxford Univ. Press.

League of Nations Treaty Series. 1924. *Treaty of Peace, at Lausanne.* Vol. 28, nos. 1–4. London: Harrison & Sons.

Lewinstein, Keith. 1994. "Notes on Eastern Hanafi Heresiography." *JAOS* 114, no. 4:583–98.

Lewis, Bernard. 1964. *The Middle East and the West.* Bloomington: Indiana Univ. Press.

———. 1968. *The Emergence of Modern Turkey.* Oxford: Oxford Univ. Press.

Lewis, Norman N. 1955. "The Frontier of Settlement in Syria, 1800–1950." *International Affairs (Royal Institute of International Affairs 1944–)* 31, no. 1:48–60.

Litvak, Meir. 1998. *Shi'i Scholars of Nineteenth-Century Iraq: The Ulama of Najaf and Karbala.* Cambridge: Cambridge Univ. Press.

Lucassen, Jan, and Erik Jan Zürcher. 1999. "Introduction: Conscription and Resistance. The Historical Context." In *Arming the State: Military Conscription in the Middle East and Central Asia, 1775–1925,* edited by Erik J. Zürcher, 1–20. London: I.B. Tauris.

Makdisi, Ussama. 2000. *The Culture of Sectarianism: Community, History, and Violence in Nineteenth-Century Ottoman Lebanon.* Berkeley and Los Angeles: Univ. of California Press.

———. 2002a. "After 1860: Debating Religion, Reform, and Nationalism in the Ottoman Empire." *IJMES* 34, no. 2:601–17.

———. 2002b. "Rethinking Ottoman Imperialism: Modernity, Violence and the Cultural Logic of Ottoman Reform." In *The Empire in the City. Arab*

Provincial Capitals in the Late Ottoman Empire, edited by Jens Hanssen, Thomas Philipp, and Stefan Weber, 29–48. Beirut: Ergon Verlag Würzburg in Kommission.

Mann, Michael. 1987. "Ruling Class Strategies and Citizenship." *Sociology* 21, no. 3:339–54.

Mardin, Şerif. 1973. "Center-Periphery Relations: A Key to Turkish Politics?" *Daedalus* 102:169–90.

Marr, Phebe. 1985. *The Modern History of Iraq.* Boulder, Colo.: Westview Press.

Marshall, T. H. 1950. *Citizenship and Social Class.* Cambridge: Cambridge Univ. Press.

———. 1965. *Class, Citizenship, and Social Development: Essays by T. H. Marshall.* New York: Anchor Books.

Massad, Joseph A. 2001. *Colonial Effects: The Making of National Identity in Jordan.* New York: Columbia Univ. Press.

Masters, Bruce. 1991. "The Treaties of Erzurum (1823 and 1848) and the Changing Status of Iranians in the Ottoman Empire." *Journal of the Society for Iranian Studies* 24, nos. 1–4:3–15.

Masud, Muhammad Khalid, Brinkley Messick, and David S. Powers, eds. 1996. *Islamic Legal Interpretation. Muftis and Their Fatwas.* Cambridge, Mass.: Harvard Univ. Press.

McCarthy, Justin. 1981. "The Population of Ottoman Syria and Iraq, 1878–1914." *Journal of the Israel Oriental Society, Asian and African Studies* 15, no. 1:3–44.

McNeill, William H., and Marilyn Robinson Waldman, eds. 1983. *The Islamic World.* Chicago: Univ. of Chicago Press.

Mélikoff, Irène. 1975. "Le Problème Kizilbas." *Turcica* 6:49–67.

———. 1982. "L'Islam Hétérodoxe En Anatolie." *Turcica* 14:142–54.

Messick, Brinkley. 1993. *The Calligraphic State: Textual Domination and History in a Muslim Society.* Berkeley and Los Angeles: Univ. of California Press.

Meyer, James H. 2007. "Immigration, Return, and the Politics of Citizenship: Russian Muslims in the Ottoman Empire, 1860–1914." *IJMES* 39, no. 1:15–32.

Moreau, Odile. 1999. "Bosnian Resistance to Conscription in the Nineteenth Century." In *Arming the State: Military Conscription in the Middle East and Central Asia, 1775–1925,* edited by Erik J. Zürcher, 129–37. London: I.B. Tauris.

Motzki, Harold. 1999. "The Role of Non-Arab Converts in the Development of Early Islamic Law." *Islamic Law and Society* 6, no. 3:293–317.

Mundy, Martha, and Richard Saumarez Smith. 2007. *Governing Property, Making the Modern State. Law, Administration and Production in Ottoman Syria.* London: I.B. Tauris.

Najmabadi, Afsaneh. 1998. *The Daughters of Quchan.* Syracuse: Syracuse Univ. Press.

Nakash, Yitzhak. 1994. *The Shi'is of Iraq.* Princeton, N.J.: Princeton Univ. Press.

Nasr, Vali. 2007. *The Shia Revival. How Conflicts Within Islam Will Shape the Future.* New York and London: W. W. Norton.

Nieuwenhuis, Tom. 1982. *Politics and Society in Early Modern Iraq. Mamluk Pashas, Tribal Shayks and Local Rule Between 1802–1831.* The Hague/Boston/London: Martinus Nijhoff Publishers.

Ochsenwald, William L. 1984. *Religion, Society and the State in Arabia: The Hijaz Under Ottoman Control, 1840–1908.* Columbus, Ohio: Ohio State Univ. Press.

Orloff, Ann Shola. 1993. "Gender and the Social Rights of Citizenship: The Comparative Analysis of Gender Relations and Welfare States." *ASR* 58, no. 3:303–28.

Owen, Roger. 1993. *The Middle East in the World Economy 1800–1914.* London: I.B. Tauris.

———. 2000. "Introduction." In *New Perspectives on Property and Land in the Middle East,* edited by Roger Owen, ix–xxiv. Cambridge, Mass.: Harvard Univ. Press.

Öz, Baki. 1995. *Alevilik ile ilgili Osmanlı Belgeleri.* Istanbul: Can Yayınları.

Özoğlu, Hakan. 2001. "'Nationalism' and Kurdish Notables in the Late Ottoman–Early Republican Era." *IJMES* 33, no. 3:383–409.

Peirce, Leslie. 2003. *Morality Tales: Law and Gender in the Ottoman Court of Aintab.* Berkeley and Los Angeles: Univ. of California Press.

Perry, John. 1979. *Karim Khan Zand: A History of Iran, 1747–1779.* Chicago: Univ. of Chicago Press.

———. 1987. "The Mamluk Paşalik of Baghdad and Ottoman-Iranian Relations in the Late Eighteenth Century." In *Studies on Ottoman Diplomatic History,* vol. 1, edited by Sinan Kuneralp, 59–70. Istanbul: The Isis Press.

Peterson, V. Spike. 1994. "Gendered Nationalism." *Peace Review* 6, no. 1:77–83.

Piscatori, James P. 1986. *Islam in a World of Nation-States.* London: Cambridge Univ. Press.

Plender, Richard. 1974. "The French Nationality Law." *International and Comparative Law Quarterly* 23, no. 4:709–47.

Pococke, Richard. 1743 and 1745. *A Description of the East and Some Other Countries.* 2 vols. London: W. Boyer.

Quataert, Donald. 2000. *The Ottoman Empire, 1700–1922.* Cambridge: Cambridge Univ. Press.

Rafeq, Abdul-Kerim. 1966. *The Province of Damascus, 1723–1783.* Beirut: Khayats.

———. 2000. "Ownership of Real Property by Foreigners in Syria, 1869–1873." In *New Perspectives on Property and Land in the Middle East,* edited by Roger Owen, 175–239. Cambridge, Mass.: Harvard Univ. Press.

Refik, Ahmed. 1932. *On Altıncı asırda, Rafızılık ve Bektaşilik.* Istanbul: Muallim Ahmet Halit Kitaphanesi.

Reid, Anthony. 1967. "Nineteenth Century Pan-Islam in Indonesia and Malaysia." *Journal of Asian Studies* 26, no. 2:267–83.

Repp, R. C. 1986. *The Müfti of Istanbul. A Study in the Development of the Ottoman Learned Hierarchy.* London: Ithaca Press.

Rochlin, S. A. 1939. "Aspects of Islam in Nineteenth-Century South Africa." *Bulletin of the School of Oriental Studies, Univ. of London* 10, no. 1:213–21.

Rogan, Eugene L. 1996. "*Aşiret Mektebi*: Abdülhamid II's School for Tribes (1892–1907)." *IJMES* 28, no. 1:83–107.

———. 1999. *Frontiers of the State in the Late Ottoman Empire. Transjordan, 1850–1921.* Cambridge: Cambridge Univ. Press.

Rosenthal, Erwin I. J. 1958. *Political Thought in Medieval Islam.* Cambridge: Cambridge Univ. Press.

Rubin, Avi. 2005. "Nation, Women, and Gender: Overview." In *Encyclopedia of Women and Islamic Culture,* edited by Suad Joseph, 331–35. Leiden, The Netherlands: E. J. Brill.

Salati, Marco. 1993. "Toleration, Persecution and Local Realities: Observations on the Shiism in the Holy Places and the *Bilad al-Sham* (Sixteenth–Seventeenth Centuries)." In *Convegno Sul Tema La Shi'a Nell'Impero Ottomano,* Roma, 15 Aprile 1991, 123–32. Rome: Accademia Nazionale Dei Lincei, Fondazione Leone Caetani.

Salzmann, Ariel. 1999. "Citizens in Search of a State: The Limits of Political Participation in the Late Ottoman Empire." In *Extending Citizenship, Reconfiguring States,* edited by Michael Hanagan and Charles Tilly, 37–66. Lanham, Md.: Rowman & Littlefield Publishers, Inc.

Saray, Prof. Dr. Mehmet. 1990. *Türk-İran Münasebetlerinde Şiiliğin Rolü.* Ankara: Türk Kültürünü Araştırma Enstitüsü Yayınları 107.

Seelye, Kate Chambers. 1919. *Moslem Schisms and Sects.* Part 1. New York: Columbia Univ. Press.

Sencer, Emre. 2004. "Balkan Nationalists in the Ottoman Parliament, 1909." *East European Quarterly* 38, no. 1:41–64.

Seton-Watson, Hugh. 1977. *Nations and States. An Enquiry into the Origins of Nations and the Politics of Nationalism.* Boulder, Colo.: Westview Press.

Shahvar, Soli. 2007. "Iron Poles, Wooden Poles: The Electric Telegraph and the Ottoman-Iranian Boundary Conflict, 1863–1865." *British Journal of Middle Eastern Studies* 34, no. 1:23–42.

Shamir, Shimon. 1963. "As'ad Pasha al-'Azm and Ottoman Rule in Damascus (1743–58)." *Bulletin of the School of Oriental and African Studies, Univ. of London* 26, no. 1:1–28.

Shaw, Stanford J. 1975. "The Nineteenth-Century Ottoman Tax Reforms and Revenue System." *IJMES* 6, no. 4:421–59.

———. 1976. *History of the Ottoman Empire and Modern Turkey,* vol. 1. Cambridge: Cambridge Univ. Press.

———. 1978. "The Ottoman Census System and Population, 1831–1914." *IJMES* 9, no. 3: 325–38.

Shaw, Stanford J., and Ezel Kural Shaw. 1977. *History of the Ottoman Empire and Modern Turkey.* Vol. 2. Cambridge: Cambridge Univ. Press.

Shields, Sarah D. 2000. *Mosul Before Iraq: Like Bees Making Five-Sided Cells.* Albany: State Univ. of New York Press.

Somel, Selçuk Akşin. 2001. *The Modernization of Public Education in the Ottoman Empire, 1839–1908.* Leiden, The Netherlands: E. J. Brill.

Sonbol, Amira El-Azhary. 2003. "'The Woman Follows the Nationality of Her Husband': Guardianship, Citizenship and Gender." *HAWWA. Journal of Women of the Middle East and the Islamic World* 1, no. 1:86–117.

Sousa, Nasim. 1933. *The Capitulatory Régime of Turkey: Its History, Origin, and Nature.* Baltimore, Md.: Johns Hopkins Press.

"Special Issue: Nationalism and the Colonial Legacy in the Middle East and Central Asia." 2002. *IJMES* 34, no. 2.

Stewart, Devin J. 1991. "A Biographical Notice on Baha' al-Din al' 'Amili (d. 1030/1621)." *JAOS* 111, no. 3:563–71.

———. 1996. "The First *Shaykh al-Islam* of the Safavid Capital Qazvin." *JAOS* 116, no. 3:387–405.

Suny, Ronald, and Geoff Eley. 1996. *Becoming National: A Reader.* New York: Oxford Univ. Press.

Tavakoli-Targhi, Mohamad. 2002. "From Patriotism to Matriotism: A Topological Study of Iranian Nationalism, 1870–1909." *IJMES* 34, no. 2:217–38.

Tekindağ, M. C. Şehabeddin. 1967. "Yeni Kaynak ve Vesikaların Isığı Altında, Yavuz Sultan Selim'in İran Seferi." *Tarih Dergisi* 17, no. 22:49–86.

Thao, Trinh Dinh. 1929. *De l'Influence du Mariage sur la Nationalité de la Femme.* Paris: Libr. Du Recueil Sirey.

Thompson, Andrew, and Ralph Fevre. 2001. "The National Question: Sociological Reflections on Nation and Nationalism." *Nations and Nationalism* 7, no. 3:297–315.

Thompson, Elizabeth. 2000. *Colonial Citizens: Republican Rights, Paternal Privilege, and Gender in French Syria and Lebanon.* New York: Columbia Univ. Press.

Tilly, Charles. 1995a. "Citizenship, Identity and Social History." *International Review of Social History* 40, supplement 3:1–17.

———. 1995b. "The Emergence of Citizenship in France and Elsewhere." *International Review of Social History* 40, supplement 3:223–36.

Tripp, Charles. 2000. *A History of Iraq.* Cambridge: Cambridge Univ. Press.

Tucker, Ernest. 1996. "The Peace Negotiations of 1736: A Conceptual Turning Point in Ottoman-Iranian Relations." *Turkish Studies Association Bulletin* 20:16–37.

Tucker, Judith. 2000. *In the House of the Law: Gender and Islamic Law in Ottoman Syria and Palestine.* Berkeley: Univ. of California Press.

Turner, Bryan S. 1990. "Outline of a Theory of Citizenship." *Sociology* 24, no. 2:189–217.

———. 2000. "Islam, Civil Society, and Citizenship: Reflections on the Sociology of Citizenship and Islamic Studies." In *Citizenship and the State in the Middle East: Approaches and Applications,* edited by Nils A. Butenschon, Uri Davis, and Manuel Hassassian, 28–48. Syracuse: Syracuse Univ. Press.

Ülker, Erol. 2005. "Contextualising 'Turkification': Nation-Building in the Late Ottoman Empire, 1908–18." *Nations and Nationalism* 11, no. 4:613–36.

Unat, İlhan. 1966. *Türk Vatandaşlık Hukuku (Metinler-Makheme Kararları).* Ankara: S. B. F. Yayını.

Van Gunsteren, Herman. 1994. "Four Conceptions of Citizenship." In *The Condition of Citizenship,* edited by Bart van Steenbergen, 36–48. London: Sage Publications.

Van Os, Nicole A. N. M. 1999. "Taking Care of Soldiers' Families: The Ottoman State and the *Muinsiz aile Maaşı*." In *Arming the State: Military Conscription in the Middle East and Central Asia, 1775–1925,* edited by Erik J. Zürcher, 95–110. London: I.B. Tauris.

Van Steenbergen, Bart. 1994. "The Condition of Citizenship: An Introduction." In *The Condition of Citizenship,* edited by Bart van Steenbergen, 1–9. London: Sage Publications.

Vogel, Ursula. 1991. "Is Citizenship Gender-Specific?" In *The Frontiers of Citizenship,* edited by Ursula Vogel and Michael Moran, 58–85. New York: St. Martin's Press.

Walby, Sylvia. 1992. "Woman and Nation." *International Journal of Comparative Sociology* 33, nos. 1–2:81–99.

———. 1994. "Is Citizenship Gendered?" *Sociology* 28, no. 2:379–95.

Wallerstein, Immanuel. 2003. "Citizens All? Citizens Some! The Making of the Citizen." *CSSH* 45, no. 4:650–79.

Walsh, J. R. 1962. "The Historiography of Ottoman-Safavid Relations." In *Historians of the Middle East,* edited by Bernard Lewis and P. M. Holt, 196–209. London: Oxford Univ. Press.

Waltz, Waldo Emerson. 1937. *The Nationality of Married Women: A Study of Domestic Policies and International Legislation.* Urbana: Univ. of Illinois Press.

Watt, W. Montgomery. 1963. "The Rafidites: A Preliminary Study." *Oriens* 16:110–21.

Weismann, Itzchak. 2007. *The Naqshbandiyya: Orthodoxy and Activism in a Worldwide Sufi Tradition.* Oxford and New York: Routledge.

White, Paul J. 1999. "Citizenship Under the Ottomans and Kemalists: How the Kurds Were Excluded." *CS* 3, no. 1:71–102.

Wildenthal, Lora. 2001. *German Women for Empire, 1884–1945.* Durham, N.C.: Duke Univ. Press.

Wilson, M. Brett. 2009. "The First Translations of the Qur'an in Modern Turkey (1924–38)." *IJMES* 41, no. 3:419–35.

Yapp, M. E. 1992. "'That Great Mass of Unmixed Mahomedanism': Reflections on the Historical Links Between the Middle East and Asia." *British Journal of Middle Eastern Studies* 19, no. 1:3–15.

Yeganeh, Naser. 1992. "Citizenship: In Modern Times (Qajar and Pahlavi Period)." In *EI,* vol. 5, edited by Ehsan Yarshater. Costa Mesa, Calif.: Mazd Publishers. Accessed at http://www.iranica.com/articles/citizenship.

Yeşil, Fatih. 2007. "Looking at the French Revolution through Ottoman Eyes: Ebubekir Ratib Efendi's Observations." *Bulletin of the School of Oriental and African Studies* 70, no. 2:283–304.

Yörükan, Prof. Yusuf Ziya. 1952. "Bir Fetva Münasebetiyle Fetva Müessesesi, Ebusuud Efendi ve Sarı Saltuk." İlahiyat Fakültesi Dergisi. Istanbul: Milli Eğitim Basımevi, 137–60.

Yüksel, Metin. 2005. "Reconstructing the History of Women in the Ottoman Empire." *International Journal of Turkish Studies* 11:49–59.

Zahedi, Ashraf. 2007. "Transnational Marriages, Gendered Citizenship, and the Dilemma of Iranian Women Married to Afghan Men." *IS* 40, no. 2:225–39.

Zarcone, Thierry. 1993. "La Communauté Iranienne D'Istanbul à la Fin du XIXe et au Début du XXe Siècle." In *Convegno Sul Tema La Shi'a Nell'Impero Ottomano,* Roma, 15 Aprile 1991, 57–83. Rome: Accademia Nazionale Dei Lincei, Fondazione Leone Caetani.

Zarcone, Thierry, and F. Zarinebaf-Shahr, eds. 1993. *Les Iraniens D'Istanbul.* Paris: Institut Français de Recherches en Iran, Institut Français d'Etudes Anatoliennes.

Zarinebaf-Shahr, Fariba. 1997. "Qizilbash `Heresy' and Rebellion in Ottoman Anatolia During the Sixteenth Century." *Anatolia Moderna, Yeni Anadolu* 7:1–15.

Zürcher, Erik Jan. 1999. "The Ottoman Conscription System in Theory and Practice, 1844–1918." In *Arming the State: Military Conscription in the Middle East and Central Asia, 1775–1925,* edited by Erik J. Zürcher, 79–94. London: I.B. Tauris.

———. 2003. *Turkey. A Modern History.* London and New York: I.B. Tauris.

Index